# Understanding and Overcoming Anxiety and Panic Attacks

## - A Guide for You and Your Caregiver

**Legal Notice**

**Authors & Publisher's note**

This publication is designed to provide information in regard to the subject matter covered.

It is sold under the understanding that the publisher and author are not engaged in rendering psychological, financial, legal, or other professional services. If expert assistance or counseling is needed, the services of a competent professional should be sought.

**For Further Help**

Though Julie & Raymond are glad to receive feedback, they cannot provide private consulting.
For further help, please consult a qualified health professional.

**Author Online!**

Raymond Le Blanc can be found at http://raymondleblanc.com

# Understanding and Overcoming Anxiety and Panic Attacks

## - A Guide for You and Your Caregiver

How to Stop
**Anxiety, Stress, Panic Attacks, Phobia & Agoraphobia**
Now

2e (revised) edition

Julie Stevenson
&
Raymond Le Blanc

**Disclaimer and terms of use agreement:**

(Please read this before using this book)

This information is not presented by a medical practitioner and is for educational and informational purposes only. The content is not intended to be a substitute for professional medical advice, diagnosis, or treatment. Always seek the advice of your physician or other qualified health provider with any questions you may have regarding a medical condition.

Never disregard professional medical advice or delay in seeking it because of something you have read.

Since natural and/or dietary supplements are not FDA approved, they must be accompanied by a two-part disclaimer on the product label: that the statement has not been evaluated by FDA and that the product is not intended to "diagnose, treat, cure or prevent any disease".

The authors and publisher of this work used their best efforts in preparing it. The authors and publisher make no representation or warranties with respect to the accuracy, applicability, fitness, or completeness of the contents of this book. The information contained in this book is strictly for educational purposes. Therefore, if you wish to apply ideas contained in this book, you are taking full responsibility for your actions.

The authors and publisher disclaim any warranties (express or implied), merchantability, or fitness for any particular purpose. The authors and publisher shall in no event be held liable to any party for any direct, indirect, punitive, special, incidental or other consequential damages arising directly or indirectly from any use of this material, which is provided "as is", and without warranties.

As always, the advice of a competent legal, tax, accounting, medical or other professional should be sought. The authors and publisher do not warrant the performance, effectiveness or applicability of any sites listed or linked to in this book. All links are for information purposes only and are not warranted for content, accuracy or any other implied or explicit purpose.

Cranendonck Coaching
Maarheeze, The Netherlands
2012

# Contents

# Chapter 1 - Introduction

A few years back, I started experiencing something I never had before.
Out of nowhere I started getting chest pains and feeling as if I was going to pass out.
I was dizzy and breaking out in a cold sweat and I could not catch my breath. I was crying hysterically because I was positive I was having a heart attack. I even convinced myself that my arm was going numb.

After nearly a week of this happening nearly every night I finally had enough and made my husband (who was my fiancé at the time) take me to the hospital at 9 p.m. at night. Never mind that he had to work early the next morning and I had to prepare for my brothers wedding which was two days away.

While at the hospital, I started to feel better, but not better enough that I wanted to leave. When I was finally brought into a room to be examined, I was so tired I just wanted to sleep but there were tests to be done. From 11 p.m. until nearly 1:30 am I was poked, prodded and pushed until they finally determined that nothing was wrong with my heart or me. My blood pressure was up and I was offered a nitro patch which I refused. By this point I had realized that I was not dying and I was certainly not having a heart attack. The doctor told me I had had a "panic attack" or an "anxiety attack" and wrote me a prescription for Xanax then sent me on my weary way.

A few weeks later the same panic happened again. My chest hurt, my pulse was racing and once again we went to the emergency room and I was convinced this was it, I was having a heart attack. Again, they told me I simply had a panic attack and it was recommended I follow up with my gp this time.

The third time it happened, my husband had enough and refused to wait with me in the emergency room. My mother came with me this time and somehow managed to convince me to leave and take a Xanax at home. She even made me breath into a paper bag to help me catch my breath. While I admit I felt like a fool doing this, it really did help me. I could not understand where this "panic" was coming from all the sudden, but I hated it every time it happened. I felt alone and scared whenever this uncontrollable feeling of something bad happening to me came over me. I felt like I had no control over it.

Pretty soon, it was starting to affect my daily life. I would lock myself in the bathroom at work because I was afraid something was happening to me and I did not want any of my coworkers to see me. I could not even go out to have something as simple as an eyebrow waxing done because I was afraid something would happen on the table. I even freaked out on the day of my bridal shower. I had such a headache that day, that I had convinced myself I was having an aneurysm. I got worse if I heard a story about someone dying suddenly and I began not sleeping at night because I was afraid I would not wake up the next morning. In fact I spent many a nights crying myself to sleep because I had convinced myself that I would not wake up. When you take into account the headaches I was having, and the constant stream of chest pains, I was a walking mess. It was certainly not a healthy way of life for me and to make it worse I kept it all bottled up inside, but I was slowly coming apart at the seams.

I finally caved in and called my doctor. Or rather I was almost forced to. My then fiancé told me that unless I took some steps to find out what was going on with me, he was not going to go through with the wedding. It was probably not the best way to get me to get help, but it did. I went in for my appointment and I told him how I was scared of a brain aneurysm, a heart attack, a blood clot, and a stroke. I fully expected my doctor to laugh or at the very least roll his eyes at my dramatics. He didn't though, in fact my doctor sent me for every test imaginable to rule out all of the above and to give me peace of mind. I had and MRI and an MRA, which incidentally sent me into even more of a panic because of the closed space you are in. I was also sent in for more blood work and an echocardiogram to rule out blood clots. Everything came back normal. My doctor hoped that with proof of a clean bill of health, my anxiety and panic would stop, but it didn't. In fact it seemed to take a turn for the worse and after my fourth appointment, he gently suggested that I meet with a therapist to get to the root of my problem.

**Tip:**
Don't hesitate to find another doctor if you feel your current doctor doesn't understand your specific needs or is uneducated about anxiety disorders. Don't let him or her intimidate you or discount how you are feeling. It took me a while to keep my appointment with the therapist. I had bad experiences in the past with them and wasn't looking forward to seeing yet another one, but the problem was becoming so severe that I could barely make it out of the house. I knew I had to do something plus it was starting to affect my relationships with other people including my employer. No one could understand what I was feeling, and some didn't even try to. I was sick of being isolated from everyone so I met with the doctor and after a few weeks, I finally had an answer about what was going on with me. I was diagnosed with a panic disorder, agoraphobia and general anxiety disorder. Now I had an answer to what was wrong, but I didn't quite understand it. I asked my doctor and was told that a panic disorder was an anxiety disorder. Anxiety? I never thought of myself as having anxiety. I mean yes, I worry a lot and maybe a little more than the next person but I didn't realize it was having such an impact on my life. I was at the beginning of my road to recovery and I wanted to get to the end as fast as possible. Before I could start though, I needed to get to the bottom of what this all was and why I was suddenly, out of nowhere, suffering from it.

**Suggestions for doctor visits:**
- Ask to be seen first or last, for shorter times of waiting in the examination room.
- Have several measures of blood pressure taken throughout the visit, in the knowledge that it will go down as you get used to being there.
- Have a glass of water available.

- Ask a staff member to check in on you while you wait for the doctor.
- Have a support person with you.

# Chapter 2 - So What Is Anxiety?

You would be surprised at how many people confuse anxiety with fear. They are two different things.

Fear is usually directed at someone, something or a specific situation. You can have a fear of certain things like bugs or animals. I for one am deadly afraid of spiders. I scream when I see a spider web because I know that means a spider is lurking somewhere but I do not associate any sort of danger with spiders. I know people who are afraid of flying (again, me too but that stems from my general anxiety disorder) and some people who are scared of heights. While being on a plane can bring on an anxiety attack, it has less to do with flying.

Anxiety is more internal. You may feel like you are losing control or as some people say "you are jumping out of your skin". You could be anxious about going to the doctors to find out test results, or you could be anxious about getting a review on an article you wrote or something you did. Usually with anxiety there is more of a physical reaction along with an emotional reaction. You may find you can't sleep while you worry or think about a coming event that is making you anxious.

Have you ever found yourself not being able to sleep the night before a big presentation, or not being able to eat the day of an interview for a job you really want? Those are all symptoms of anxiety. Granted, it is not the type of anxiety that will send you into some sort of attack, but it is anxiety just the same.

Anxiety is a part of life and it is normal to experience some form of anxiety at some point or another. In fact, I would be worried if you didn't experience some form of anxiety at one point or another. Children even experience some form of anxiety at some point or another. They are anxious about starting school, or camp, etc.

Now anxiety and anxiety disorders are two different things. An anxiety disorder is a more intense feeling of anxiety (for example, panic attacks) that lasts for quite some time. Normally your anxiety will go away after the event or situation is over and done with. When you have an anxiety disorder, you may have the anxiety for months on end and the disorder could lead to phobias or fears that affect your life. This is exactly what happened to me. I was so anxious of having the same experience as my father that I was never fully comfortable away from my loved ones. Even now, when I have my GAD (Generalized Anxiety Disorder) and my attacks under control, I still find myself having flare-ups if my husband and daughter are away from me for too long.

Another distinction between anxiety and anxiety disorder is the fact that the latter can lead to phobias that interfere with your life. There are several anxiety disorders. There is Generalized Anxiety Disorder, Panic Disorder, Obsessive-Compulsive disorder, post-traumatic stress disorder, agoraphobia and social phobia to name a few.

I found out that anxiety disorders are the number one mental health problem among American women and the second only to alcohol and drug abuse among men. Roughly 15 percent of the US population, or nearly 40 million people, have suffered from panic attacks, phobias, or other anxiety disorders in the past year. Even more disturbing is the fact that nearly a quarter of the adult population will suffer from an anxiety attack at some time during their life! Yet only a small proportion of these people receive treatment.

**Stages in Anxiety**:
**Mild**
Tension of day-to-day living; you have a better ability to interpret or become aware of something through your senses (you have an alert perceptual field); a mild stage of anxiety can motivate learning. Example: anxiety felt when missing the bus.
**Moderate**
Focus is on immediate concerns: perceptual field is narrowed; you show selective inattention. Example: anxiety felt when taking an exam.
**Severe**
Focus is on a specific detail; perceptual field is greatly reduced. Example: anxiety felt when witnessing a car accident.
**Panic**
You experience a sense of awe, dread, and/or terror; you lose control; there is a disorganization of the personality. Example: anxiety felt when experiencing an earthquake and being unable to cope.

Before focusing on the different types of anxiety disorders I'll first take a closer look at the differences between stress and anxiety.

## *Stress Or Anxiety*

Contrary to popular belief, there is a difference between stress and anxiety.

An existing stress-causing factor or stressor causes stress. Anxiety is stress that continues after that stressor is gone. Stress can come from any situation or thought that makes you feel frustrated, angry, nervous, or even anxious. What is stressful to one person is not necessarily stressful to another.

Anxiety is a feeling of apprehension or fear and is almost always accompanied by feelings of impending doom. The source of this uneasiness is not always known or recognized, which can add to the distress you feel.

Stress is the way our bodies and minds react to something which upsets our normal balance in life; an example of stress is the response we feel when we are frightened or threatened. During stressful events our adrenal glands release adrenaline, a hormone that activates our body's defense mechanisms causing our hearts to pound, blood pressure to rise, muscles to tense, and the pupils of our eyes to dilate. A principal signal of increased stress is an escalation in your pulse rate; however, a normal pulse rate doesn't necessarily mean you are not stressed. Constant aches and pains, palpitations, anxiety, chronic fatigue, crying, over or under-eating, frequent infections, and a decrease in your sexual desire are signs you may notice which suggest you may be under stress. Of course, every time we are under stress, we do not react to such an extreme and we are not always under such great duress or fear every time we are confronted with a stressful situation.

Some people are more susceptible than others to stress; for some, even ordinary daily decisions seem insurmountable. Deciding what to have for dinner or what to buy at the store, is a seemingly, monumental dilemma for them. On the other hand, there are those people, who seem to thrive under stress by becoming highly productive being driven by the force of pressure.

Research shows women with children have higher levels of stress related hormones in their blood than women without children. Does this mean women without children don't experience stress? Absolutely not! It means that women without children may not experience stress as often or to the same degree as women with children do. It's important for women with children, to schedule time for yourself; you will be in a better frame of mind to help your children and meet the daily challenge of being a parent, once your stress level is reduced.

Anxiety, on the other hand, is a feeling of unease. Everybody experiences it when faced with a stressful situation, for example before an exam or an interview, or during a worrying time such as illness. It is normal to feel anxious when facing something difficult or dangerous and mild anxiety can be a positive and useful experience.

However, for many people, anxiety interferes with normal life. Excessive anxiety is often associated with other psychiatric conditions, such as depression. Anxiety is considered abnormal when it is prolonged or severe, it happens in the absence of a stressful event, or it is interfering with everyday activities such as going to work.

The physical symptoms of anxiety are caused by the brain sending messages to parts of the body to prepare for the "fight or flight" response. The heart, lungs and other parts of the body work faster. The brain also releases stress hormones, including adrenaline.

## Common indicators of excessive anxiety include:
- Diarrhea
- Dry mouth
- Rapid heartbeat or palpitations
- Insomnia
- Irritability or anger
- Inability to concentrate
- Fear of being "crazy"
- Feeling unreal and not in control of your actions which is called depersonalization

**Anxiety can be brought on in many ways.**
Obviously, the presence of stress in your life can make you have anxious thoughts. Many people who suffer from anxiety disorders occupy their minds with excessive worry. This can be worry about anything from health matters to job problems to world issues.

Certain drugs, both recreational and medicinal, can also lead to symptoms of anxiety because of either side effects or withdrawal from the drug. Such drugs include caffeine, alcohol, nicotine, cold remedies, and decongestants, bronchodilators for asthma, tricyclic antidepressants, cocaine, amphetamines, diet pills, ADHD medications, and thyroid medications. A poor diet can also contribute to stress or anxiety -- for example, low levels of vitamin B12.

Performance anxiety is related to specific situations, like taking a test or making a presentation in public.

Post-traumatic stress disorder (PTSD) is a stress disorder that develops after a traumatic event like war, physical or sexual assault, or a natural disaster. In very rare cases, a tumor of the adrenal gland may be the cause of anxiety. This happens because of an overproduction of hormones responsible for the feelings and symptoms of anxiety.

## *Quiz Time!*
This information comes from reliable sources and *isn't meant to be a complete diagnostic tool in any way.*

Ask yourself the following:
- ✓ Do you worry constantly and cycle with negative self-talk?
- ✓ Do you have difficulty concentrating?
- ✓ Do you get mad and react easily?
- ✓ Do you have recurring neck or headaches?
- ✓ Do you grind your teeth?
- ✓ Do you frequently feel overwhelmed, anxious or depressed?
- ✓ Do you feed your stress with unhealthy habits-eating or drinking excessively, smoking, arguing, or avoiding yourself and life in other ways?
- ✓ Do small pleasures fail to satisfy you?
- ✓ Do you experience flashes of anger over a minor problem?

If you can answer "Yes" to most of these questions, then you do have excessive stress in your life. The good news is that you can learn many valuable techniques to cope with that stress. But we'll get to that later!

Let's move on to anxiety.
- ✓ Do you experience shortness of breath, heart palpitation or shaking while at rest?
- ✓ Do you have a fear of losing control or going crazy?
- ✓ Do you avoid social situations because of fear?
- ✓ Do you have fears of specific objects?
- ✓ Do you fear that you will be in a place or situation from which you cannot escape?

- ✓ Do you feel afraid of leaving your home?
- ✓ Do you have recurrent thoughts or images that refuse to go away?
- ✓ Do you feel compelled to perform certain activities repeatedly?
- ✓ Do you persistently relive an upsetting event from the past?

Answering "Yes" to more than four of these questions can indicate an anxiety disorder.

You don't have to be a victim of stress and anxiety. Not taking in anything you cannot handle will be a lot of help. Learn your limitations and stick to it. Do not over exert yourself. Just try to go over the border an inch at a time. You can lead a productive successful and fulfilling life and career without the need to endanger your health. If not, you are not only killing yourself, you are also driving your family and friends and all the people around you away from you.

Stress is a natural part of life. It can be both physical and mental and much of it can come from everyday pressures. Everyone handles stress differently, some better than others. Left unchecked, however, stress can cause physical, emotional, and behavioral disorders which can affect your health, vitality, and peace-of-mind, as well as personal and professional relationships. As we've said, stress and anxiety can lead to panic attacks. Speaking from experience, I can tell you that having a panic attack can be a serious situation. I'll come to that later.

## *Panic Attacks*

You would be surprised at how many people go to the hospital emergency room completely sure that they're having a heart attack only to find out that it's a panic attack. They're that intense!

It's very difficult for your loved ones to imagine or even understand what you are going through when you have a panic attack. They may lose patience with you, tell you to "get over it", or think you're faking. It may help if you show them the following scenario.

You are standing in line at the grocery store. It's been a long wait but there's only one customer to go before you make it to the cashier. Wait, what was that? An unpleasant feeling forms in your throat, your chest feels tighter, now a sudden shortness of breath, and what do you know—your heart skips a beat. "Please, God, not here." You make a quick scan of the territory—is it threatening? Four unfriendly faces are behind you and one person is in front. Pins and needles seem to prick you through your left arm, you feel slightly dizzy, and then the explosion of fear as you dread the worst. You are about to have a panic attack. There is no doubt in your mind now that this is going to be a big one. Okay, time for you to focus. You know how to deal with this – at least you hope you do! Start breathing deeply - in through the nose, out through the mouth. Think relaxing thoughts, and again, while breathing in, think "Relax," and then breathe out. But it doesn't seem to be having any positive effect; in fact, just concentrating on breathing is making you feel self-conscious and more

15

uptight. Maybe if you just try to relax your muscles. Tense both shoulders, hold for 10 seconds, then release. Try it again. Nope, still no difference. The anxiety is getting worse and the very fact that you are out of coping techniques worsens your panic. If only your family, or a close friend were beside you so you could feel more confident in dealing with this situation. Now, the adrenaline is really pumping through your system, your body is tingling with uncomfortable sensations, and now the dreaded feeling of losing complete control engulfs your emotions. No one around you has any idea of the sheer terror you are experiencing. For them, it's just a regular day and another frustratingly slow line at the grocery store. You realize you are out of options. It's time to run. You excuse yourself from the line looking embarrassed, as now it is your turn to pay. The cashier is looking bewildered as you leave your shopping behind and stroll towards the door. There is no time for excuses—you need to be alone. You leave the supermarket and get into your car to ride it out alone. You wonder whether or not this one was the big one. The one you fear will push you over the edge mentally and physically. Ten minutes later the panic subsides. It's only 11:00 in the morning, how in the world can you make it through the rest of your day?

If you suffer from panic or anxiety attacks, the above scenario probably sounds very familiar. It may have even induced feelings of anxiety and panic just reading it. In fact, it was difficult for me just to write it! The particular situations that trigger your panic and anxiety may differ. Maybe the bodily sensations are a little different.

What's important to realize is that panic attacks are very real to the people who are having them and they should never be pushed off to the side. I remember one evening at home when I was by myself watching one of my favorite television programs. I thought I was in a safe place. There was no obvious trigger and I felt completely relaxed. Out of nowhere, I began having symptoms of a panic attack. The four walls of my living room were closing in around me. I couldn't breathe and felt like I was dying. I stepped out on my front porch for some fresh air and began deep breathing exercises. The symptoms eventually went away, but it left me wondering why exactly I had that attack.

There was no obvious reason, no stressful situation, and no indicator that a panic attack might be impending. That's the strange thing about panic. Sometimes your mind can play tricks on you. Even when you think you're in no danger of having a panic attack, your brain might be feeling differently. That's the scary part.

The good part is that there are ways you can combat panic attacks and cope much better when you find yourself in that situation.

### Visit A Doctor If Possible
A visit to the doctor isn't always possible, but if it is, you should go.

When you're having panic attacks, they may make you feel as though there is something terrible wrong with you physically. When you feel like something is grievously wrong with you, the anxiety tends to spiral out of control. The more you worry about your health, the worse it gets, and the worse it gets, the more you worry.

When you visit a doctor, the doctor can help assure you that nothing is physically wrong with you. While it may be extremely disturbing to feel so out of control of your own body, knowing the illness isn't physical can be comforting.

If you feel you are at risk of imminent death, you are obviously going to feel extremely anxious. This type of anxiety is a nightmare for people who suffer from panic attacks. By getting affirmation from a medical professional that you aren't having a heart attack or some other life threatening illness, you will be able to use that to calm yourself down when panic strikes.

## Who Suffers From Anxiety?

People you would never suspect in a million years! In fact, Anxiety is such a widespread disorder that virtually anyone can suffer from it. Your uncle Buddy, your Grandma Jean, your sister Annie, your neighbor Joe, your best friend Patti, or your brother George.
But, because Anxiety is one of those 'sweep it under the carpet', "embarrassment-type-I-think-I-might-be-going-crazy" disorders, people don't like to talk about it. Or admit they are long time sufferers.

Let us not forget also that Anxiety is believed to be an inherited disorder, although your mother or father may not show the outward symptoms of it. Remember, this is an embarrassment disorder, or one that makes the sufferer believe they are, or are going, crazy.

However, not every person who has experienced an Anxiety attack will develop a full blown disorder, but don't discount the fact that potentially they could.

### Even Hollywood Stars Can Have Panic Disorders

Often, people will look at Hollywood stars from a distance, and wish that they were so perfect and glamorous. But what people forget is that Hollywood stars are, after all, just people. They are no more immune to the problems that plague people than the rest of us are. And panic disorders are no exception.

All sorts of people can have panic disorders. Men, women, children, business executives, and yes, Hollywood stars. It can be interesting to read about Hollywood stars and their battles with panic disorders. As you can imagine, having a panic disorder such as stage fright can cause serious problems for a person whose career is based on appearing in front of large groups of people. The image any Hollywood star wants to project is that of calm confidence, and having a panic attack that is caught on film can shatter that image. But panic attacks can happen anywhere, anytime. Some Hollywood stars have admitted to having panic attacks: Onstage, and forgetting lines or lyrics. On an airplane. Some recollect having panic attacks even as a teenager. Panic attacks caused by their status as celebrities. Panic attacks brought on by the constant scrutiny and photographs of paparazzi.

In general, panic disorders are not particularly tied to any one event. There are many cases of Hollywood stars that have panic attacks, but never onstage, or not particularly tied to being onstage. Stage fright (the disorder) is a kind of anxiety disorder, not a panic disorder. The defining trait of panic disorders as opposed to anxiety disorders are that panic attacks can happen anywhere, anytime. So, while a Hollywood star may have a panic attack onstage, it's not because they were onstage. It just happened to occur while they were onstage. It is good that Hollywood stars are willing to share their experiences fighting panic disorders. Their stories and how they deal with their panic disorder can help all people with panic disorders learn to cope. People are usually embarrassed by their panic disorder, and having someone so very much in the public eye come out and tell their experiences dealing with panic disorders can lessen that feeling.

Ignoring your condition is the worst thing you can do. Seek treatment, and realize it is nothing to be embarrassed about. 40 million Americans each year are treated for anxiety and panic disorders, so you are far from alone. And if a Hollywood star, who depends on their public image more than most, can come out and tell the world that they have a panic disorder, you should be able to as well.

# Chapter 3 - Types Of Anxiety Disorders

The information provided in this chapter might be overwhelming.
That's why I'll start to provide you with a summary of major anxiety Disorders.

### General Anxiety Disorder
Definition: Anxiety focused on various life events or activities.
Symptoms: Restlessness, fatigue, difficulty in concentrating, irritability, muscle tension, sleep problems.

### Panic Disorder
Definition: Discrete episodes of intense anxiety that begin abruptly and reach a peak within about 10 minutes.
Symptoms: Palpitations, sweating, trembling, shortness of breath, sensation of choking, chest pain, nausea, dizziness, fear of losing control, fear of dying, sense of altered reality.

### Agoraphobia
Definition: Acute anxiety in crowds; fear of being alone; fear in any physical setting from which the individual may have trouble escaping.
Symptoms: Intense feelings of anxiety or fear of losing control that results in either refraining from going out or avoiding situations that may cause anxiety.

### Phobia
Definition: Persistent, excessive, or unreasonable fear of a specific object or situation (examples: elevators, airplanes, dogs, spiders, injections, tunnels).
Symptoms: Fears that interfere markedly with life activities.

### Obsessive-Compulsive Disorder
Definition: Happening of recurrent thoughts, images, or impulses that are intrusive and inappropriate, causing anxiety (obsession) and coupled with repetitive actions or behaviors performed to reduce the anxiety (compulsions).
Symptoms: Individual recognizes that this thoughts and/or behaviors are unreasonable; for example, the person who wishes to stop checking and rechecking an alarm clock at night but feels unable to stop the repetitive behavior.

### Post traumatic-stress disorder
Definition: After exposure to a significant, life threatening event, the experience of anxiety symptoms in which the event is re-experienced through recollections.
Symptoms: Recurrent recollections, dreams, hallucinatory-like flashbacks, impairment of social functioning.

## *General Anxiety Disorder*

If you have been diagnosed with GAD (General Anxiety Disorder), it means that you have chronic anxiety that lasts for at least six months. Chances are you might have no idea what it is you are so worried about but everyday you are filled with worry and tension. The key is you don't have as many of the other physical symptoms that are associated with other panic disorders. Most doctors state that, to diagnose someone with GAD, your anxiety and worry focuses on two or more stressful life situations like your health or your relationships for most of the time during a six-month period. Essentially you have no control over these worries.

Besides worrying, people with GAD usually experience at least three of these symptoms though not every single day:
- Restlessness
- Getting tired easily
- Hard time concentrating
- Irritability
- Muscle tension
- Insomnia

Besides these main symptoms, some sufferers of GAD also complain of frequent headaches, difficulty swallowing, trembling, and sometimes hot flashes.
If you suffer from GAD, you are not alone. Statistics show that millions of adults suffer from GAD. It can start at any age. Children and teens have been diagnosed also with GAD because they worry about school performance or sports performances.

If you have GAD chances are, you can still function in your everyday life. This disorder is a heightened sense of anxiety or worry experienced on a daily basis. It is a chronic disorder that is continuous throughout the sufferers day. They experience difficulty concentrating or constant, excessive worry about every day concerns with an inability to control those overwhelming feelings of worry. Symptoms can also include increased nervousness, irritability, fatigue or restlessness. While not as extreme a condition such as Anxiety/Panic Disorder, it is still a serious illness that requires professional treatment from a qualified health care provider or counselor.

## *Panic Disorder*

Your heart starts to pound. . . You begin to feel dizzy or faint. . . You experience shortness of breath. . . You feel tingling or numbness in your hands and feet. . . You start to feel pressure in your chest. . . You think you may be dying or at the least having a heart attack.. . You think you may be going crazy. . . But you're not!

These are the classic symptoms of a Panic Attack. Millions of people scattered about the United States, not to mention other countries across the world, have them every single day. You may be one of them. Or you may know someone who is battling with this affliction.

This is the form of the disorder that brings on sudden attacks that paralyze you with fear for no apparent reason. Of course there are underlying factors that cause these attacks, however, the sufferer rarely knows what those are, unless they seek professional help from a family physician or a clinical specialist who are equipped to deal with this type of disorder.

One of the unfortunate outcomes from suffering from excessive stress and apprehension is a physical reaction of your body to the situation. It's like your body is telling you that you need to rest for a moment. Except when you're having a panic attack, it's anything but restful. As I said earlier, I would start getting chest pains, heart palpitations and fears of going crazy usually out of the blue. I was a classic example of someone suffering from Panic Disorder. Other symptoms that come with the panic attacks associated with panic disorders are

- Dizziness and faintness
- Trembling
- Feeling of choking
- Sweating
- Stomach pains, nausea
- Feeling of unreality
- Tingling in hands and feet
- Hot and cold flashes
- Fears of going crazy
- Fears of dying.

Now most of these are common responses for our "flight or fight" instinct. The biggest difference is that usually a certain danger will trigger these feelings in us, while a panic attack will come out of nowhere. Panic attacks can be scary because the symptoms can be similar to a heart attack or at least what we think having a heart attack would be like. Most people who experience a panic attack for the first time will wind up seeking medical advice.

Anxiety/Panic Disorder is often connected with other serious disorders such as depression. Due to the fact that the attacks associated with this disorder are such terrifying events, the sufferer may make several trips to the local emergency room not really knowing the true cause as it may be difficult to get a correct diagnosis at first. This disorder can be very debilitating to the sufferer and can extremely hinder their daily activities. If a sufferer experiences an attack while driving, they will avoid driving to avoid having another attack. This can be true of any type of daily activity such as grocery shopping, doing dishes, watching television, etc. However, this form of disorder is the most treatable of all the Anxiety Disorders, and so an individual experiencing, or believe he is experiencing symptoms of this disorder should seek help and effective treatment through their chosen health care professional.

## Agoraphobia

This is perhaps the most common anxiety disorder. It is estimated that 1 out of every 20 people suffer from some form of Agoraphobia. Alcoholism is the only other disorder in America that affects more people than agoraphobia. The textbook definition of agoraphobia means fear of open spaces but it is really the fear of panic attacks. This means that most people with agoraphobia avoid places where they might not be able to leave easily if they have a panic attack and avoid possible embarrassment. The panic attack isn't only scary most of the time but what other people might think is scary as well.

My agoraphobia kept me out of many public places when I was at my lowest. I lost count of how many times I had almost finished my grocery shopping only to feel the all too familiar heart pounding and pulse racing sensations and I would bolt from the store and arrive back home empty handed but shaking from fear. I learned that one of the most common features about agoraphobia is anxiety about being far away from home or a safe person. This was true for me. I hated to be away from my husband and felt like something was wrong if I wasn't with him. I still to this day get nervous if I'm away from him or my daughter.

Agoraphobia usually comes with a panic disorder. A panic disorder is when you have no idea why a panic attack happens, but once you become aware that these attacks can tend to happen more when you are alone or in small spaces you will find that you don't want to be alone.

Not every person who has a panic disorder will develop agoraphobia, nor will every two people have the same severity of it. However it is known that it can be caused by a combination of heredity and environment. When I say heredity I mean that it can be a learned trait. In fact children whose parents are agoraphobic have a higher risk of developing it themselves because it is what they have learned. I remember wondering when and where in the world did I develop a panic disorder. In nearly 28 years, I have never had one before and it wasn't until my diagnosis that I dove into learning all I could about this one disorder.

Usually the causes are heredity, chemical imbalances and personal stress. One of the most effective treatments for panic attacks is to begin to realize the signs of an oncoming panic attack and being able to ride the attack out.
We'll talk more about that later.

## *Phobias*

This category involves a strong, irrational fear and avoidance of an object or situation. The person knows the fear is irrational, yet the anxiety remains.

Phobic disorders differ from generalized anxiety disorders and panic disorders because there is a specific stimulus or situation that elicits a strong fear response. A person suffering from a phobia of spiders might feel so frightened by a spider that he or she would try to jump out of a speeding car to get away from one. People with phobias have especially powerful imaginations, so they vividly anticipate terrifying consequences from encountering such feared objects as knives, bridges, blood, enclosed places, certain animals or situations. These individuals generally recognize that their fears are excessive and unreasonable but are generally unable to control their anxiety.

## Social Phobia / Social anxiety disorder

This is another common anxiety disorder and it involves the fear of embarrassment in public situations. Now you may think that everyone at one point or another suffers from some sort of nervousness when it comes to being in a social situation or a performance situation. I myself get nervous before big gatherings and tend to get a little crazy every time I was due on stage. The difference is these feelings passed.

If you suffer from social phobia, your feelings are a little deeper. Your worry is you will be judged on everything you say and do. If you do something wrong you will be looked at as anxious, weak or even crazy. The most common fear of social phobia is speaking in public and it can affect performers, speakers and anyone whose job requires them to make presentations. Other social phobias are

- Fear of blushing in public
- Fear of being watched at work
- Fear of using public toilets
- Fear of crowds
- Fear of taking examinations

Because social phobias are so common, some doctors will only give an actual diagnosis of social phobia only if your avoidance is interfering with work, social activities or relationships. Also, if you suffer from panic attacks from the sheer thought of doing something in public, you are probably suffering from social phobia.

The biggest difference between panic attacks and panic attacks brought on by social phobia is that social phobia panic attacks stem from your fear of being humiliated rather than feeling trapped or fearing for your life. Also these attacks do not come out of the blue but rather when you are faced with a certain type of social situation.

Usually medications can be prescribed for social phobia. People have benefited from taking medication such as Paxil to treat their phobia but most people benefit more from social skills training. They relearn basic social skills like smiling and making eye contact along with active listening.
This type of disorder more commonly strikes when a sufferer is placed within a social setting.
It is also referred to as Social Phobia and can be a very traumatic and debilitating disorder making it near impossible for one afflicted with it to be comfortable at any social gathering. This includes everyday functions such as attending class, going out to dinner at a restaurant, or even going to work. The person suffering from this disorder has strong self-conscious issues and may often feel as if they are not welcome, or really a part of the social setting. They feel as if they are constantly being judged or watched by others for no apparent reason other than those things they themselves feel self-conscious about.
The social settings can be those that occur on a daily basis, or those that are rare occurrences, such as a party, public speaking events, etc. Oftentimes, the

sufferer will experience any of the following symptoms when placed in social gatherings: profuse sweating, trembling or shaking, feeling sick to their stomachs, inability to speak, or blushing.

A person suffering from this type of disorder can become so upset by an upcoming social event that it will plague them for weeks in advance working them into an anxious frenzy by the time the event finally comes around. In an attempt to 'self-medicate', a person experiencing this disorder will often times turn to alcohol or 'street' drugs to cope which leads to more disorders springing up. This disorder usually happens sometime during early childhood or adolescence and continues on throughout adulthood. Treatment for this disorder can be accomplished through careful and consistent counseling and medication.

## *Specific Phobia*

This category involves a strong, irrational fear and avoidance of an object or situation. The person knows the fear is irrational, yet the anxiety remains. Phobic disorders differ from generalized anxiety disorders and panic disorders because there is a specific stimulus or situation that elicits a strong fear response. A person suffering from a phobia of spiders might feel so frightened by a spider that he or she would try to jump out of a speeding car to get away from one.

People with phobias have especially powerful imaginations, so they vividly anticipate terrifying results from facing such feared objects as knives, bridges, blood, enclosed places, certain animals or situations. These individuals recognize that their fears are excessive and unreasonable but are generally unable to control their anxiety.

## *Obsessive Compulsive Disorder*

I'm sure all of us know at least one person who we might have joked at one point or another that they are obsessive compulsive. It might be the neat freak that we know or the person who keeps hand sanitizer at their desk. But obsessive compulsive is a real disease.

Let's break it down to what the words obsessive compulsive mean. Obsessive are recurring ideas, thoughts and images that may seem senseless but still manage to enter your mind. You realize that they are irrational but you still are constantly thinking about them. You may spend hours or days thinking about them even though you do not want to. Compulsions are rituals that you perform to dispel the anxiety brought up by the obsessions. If you constantly obsess about if you locked your door or not, you will probably find yourself checking your locks constantly if you have a compulsion about it. The thing about obsessive compulsions is that you know they are unreasonable yet you still find the need to do it. The most common compulsions are washing, checking and counting.

Washers are obsessed with avoiding contamination and may spend hours a day showering and washing their hands. They may avoid doorknobs, handshakes or touching anything that might have come into contact with something toxic. Women tend to be a lot more of the washer types while men are the checkers.

A checker will check to see if their door is closed and locked constantly because of an obsession of being robbed, they are constantly checking their stoves to make sure no burners are left on due to obsessions about a fire happening to them. While it is normal to have some obsessions about this, I for one am always checking to make sure I locked my doors but it is mainly because I can be more absent minded than anything else.

Lastly you have the counting obsession which is when a person must count up to a certain number or repeat a certain word so many times to get rid of anxiety. Or they must count to a certain number to brush their teeth, their hair or even wash their hands. Other symptoms of it can be having to stick to personal rules of how to walk, and eat. Some people have to cut their food into the right amount of pieces before they can eat it.

A very early onset of OCD (Obsessive Compulsive Disorder) is early childhood but most of the time it is missed because no one thinks that OCD is a possibility this young.

Usually the most effective way to manage OCD is medication and behavioral therapy.

## *Post Traumatic Stress Disorder*

I think this is the most talked about anxiety disorder. This can occur after a sufferer has witnessed or experienced a highly traumatic event such as a criminal assault, a bad accident, war, child abuse or a naturally occurring or human-inflicted disaster. Many servicemen and women have reported suffering from its symptoms which include flashbacks, nightmares, overwhelming anger or depression as well as feeling irritable and easily distracted.

Families of victims can also develop this disorder. You constantly hear about people suffering from Post Traumatic Stress. For those of you who might not know exactly what it is, it is a disorder that can occur in anyone regardless of age, after they have experienced a severe trauma that is outside their threshold to handle. Many soldiers suffer from post traumatic stress because of what they have seen overseas. It has been reported that some survivors of the 9-11 attacks on the World Trade Center and the Pentagon suffer from PTSD (Post Traumatic Stress Disorder) as well as survivors of Hurricane Katrina.

PTSD can affect anyone who has been involved in any of the following: a car crash, a plane crash, rape attack or any other violent crime against themselves or their family. To be diagnosed with PTSD you usually have most if not all of the following symptoms for at least a month.
- Repetitive, distressing thoughts about the trauma

- Nightmares about the experience
- Reliving the experience through flashbacks
- Avoidance of thoughts or feelings from the experience
- Avoidance of activities that are associated with the experience
- Being out of touch with your feelings
- Feelings of detachment from others
- Losing interest in things you used to enjoy
- Increased anxiety

For example some people who developed PTSD after a serious car accident have a sudden phobia about driving or even getting into a car.

Sufferers of PTSD often state they are depressed as well and sometimes lash out at those closest to them. Again therapy and medication is the best treatment for this disorder.

## Child Anxiety Attacks

Anxiety disorders can affect people of all walks of life, ethnic backgrounds, and age groups.

Child anxiety attacks are not only possible, they are probably happening more often than doctors realize. This condition seems to especially affect teenagers and can persist into young adulthood.

### Symptoms of a Child Anxiety Attack

The symptoms of a child anxiety attack are generally the same as an adult having an anxiety attack would feel. A child anxiety attack may start with a psychological symptom, such as a persistent and strong feeling of dread or fear. This is then followed by physical symptoms, the same as an adult would experience: racing heart, chest discomfort, numbness or tingling in the extremities, etcetera. Also common among child anxiety sufferers are diarrhea, stomach pain, headaches, nausea, and shortness of breath.

### Effects of Child Anxiety Attacks

Even though anxiety attacks generally don't cause any direct physical damage, the effects on a child's psyche can be very noticeable. Children suffering from child anxiety attacks often have trouble concentrating in school, and may show an overall lower ability to learn or make decisions. Often child anxiety attacks can be triggered by social situations, so the child may attempt to isolate himself to try and avoid triggering a child anxiety attack.

There are many different kinds of child anxiety disorders: Obsessive Compulsive Disorder (OCD), acute stress disorder, social or general phobias, Generalized Anxiety Disorder, and adjustment disorders with anxiety, to name just a few. Many of these involve child anxiety disorders that focus on specific situations, people, objects, et cetera.

**Helping Your Child**

If your child is experiencing anything that you suspect may be child anxiety attacks, you should take them to see a doctor. He will be able to diagnose whether there is anything physically wrong, and if not, will be able to recommend some treatments that can help. Generally, child anxiety is treated the same way as adult anxiety: with medication and therapy.

Your doctor will be able to prescribe medications that will help control your child's anxiety attacks. The therapy will help them to overcome the fears that are at the root of the child anxiety attacks. At home, try and keep your child's life as stress-free as possible. Don't be overbearing or put too much pressure on them to be perfect. Don't argue with your husband or wife where they can hear you. Stress from a bad home life can really take its toll on a child's mind. Rather, make sure they feel loved and secure, and that they know they will always be loved even if they don't get that "A". You'll find that reducing the stress your child feels can help their recovery quite a bit.

## *Panic Disorders In Adolescents*

It can turn out to be a difficult task to make a diagnosis of panic disorders in the adolescents, as their behavior is very unpredictable. They do not communicate well with people and thus the parents find it very difficult to know what exactly is wrong with their kids. The parents consequently come to know this only when their kids undergo a panic attack. The adolescents are always troublesome and hard to put up with during their anxiety, panic or worry.

Life is hard-hitting without having to be a teenager. The roles of hormones are intense and the adolescent brain fabricates an excess of many chemicals.

The good news is that this disorder can be treated and is curable.

Some of the symptoms the adolescents (suffering from this disorder), undergo usually are:

- Increase in the heart beat count
- Wooziness
- Difficulty in breathing
- Wobbliness
- Perplexity

This disorder if present among the adolescents may also produce other behavioral problems. E.g.: The teenager may refuse to mingle with people and may not get out of the house. They will have trepidation of associating as they would not want to get a panic attack when facing their friends. These teenagers are vulnerable to depression too.

They might also have problems or troubles at their school and often unnecessary fears. The panic disorders are difficult to be identified in the teenagers, but if you recognize the problem it will not be a difficult task to address the trouble. When you suspect that an adolescent is suffering from this disorder then you must not hesitate to take him or her to a medical doctor for physical evaluation. If there are no symptoms found for the panic attacks then you must visit a psychologist.

When parents try to help their children to overcome this problem they must bear in mind the child's interpretation of life. An adolescent may be anxious for various reasons. They may feel frustration with their lives or have problems with low self-esteem. To name just a few of the reasons for panic attacks in youngsters.
You might see your child as vigorous and pretty but your child may not feel the same.

There are treatments available to cure the disorder among adolescents. These include physical, mental, spiritual and cognitive treatments. These teenagers learn to manage the disorder and change their life style and way of thinking so as to reduce their tendency of worry. They can be cured with proper treatments.

# Chapter 4 - Anxiety Diagnosis

Anxiety disorders are often exhausting chronic conditions, which can be present from an early age or begin suddenly after a triggering event. They are prone to flare up at times of high stress.

A good assessment is essential for the first diagnosis of an anxiety disorder, preferably using a standardized interview or questionnaire procedure alongside expert evaluation and the views of the affected person. There should be a medical examination to identify possible medical conditions that can cause the symptoms of anxiety.

A family history of anxiety disorders is often suggestive of the possibility of an anxiety disorder. Although rare, it is important to exclude the possibility of a neuroendocrine tumor of the medulla of the adrenal glands. The presence of a such a tumor is normally accompanied by paroxysms of headache, sweating, palpitations, and hypertension. It is important to note that a patient with an anxiety disorder will often display symptoms of Clinical Depression and vice versa. Rarely does a patient show symptoms of only one or the other.

**Tip:**
Get a complete physical, including a check of your thyroid, blood iron levels and vestibular system. This can be a big help in ruling out some of your biggest fears. Once you have had your physical, remind yourself that you are healthy.

## *Self Tests*

When it comes to making a diagnosis consulting your doctor is usually the best place to start. Your doctor will take a careful history, perform a physical examination, and order laboratory tests as needed.
If you have another medical condition that you know about, there may be an overlap of signs and symptoms between what is old and what is new.
Just determining that anxiety is psychological does not immediately identify the ultimate cause. Often, finding out the cause requires involving a psychiatrist, clinical psychologist, or other mental-health professional.

Nevertheless if you think you might be a victim of an anxiety disorder you might want to do a self-test.

If you find it difficult to discuss your anxiety with your doctor it might be helpful to score a self-test (on the internet) and print the score. You can use this score to discuss your worries with the doctor. There are several tests you can find on the Internet. Just search for "anxiety tests" using your favorite search engine.

**For instance:**
http://tinyurl.com/36kmdd This test is designed to evaluate your general level of anxiety. Examine the statements in the test and point out how often you feel that way.

http://tinyurl.com/2lj8l6 This test will discover whether you should consider seeking help, and to what degree. For each statement in the questionnaire, you should indicate how often you feel that way. After finishing the test, you will receive a Snapshot Report with an introduction, a graph and a personalized interpretation for one of your test scores. You will then have the choice to buy the full results.

Note: Don't be alarmed by these strange looking web site addresses. I have used them so you don't have to manually copy the long urls.

**Warning**:
In no way should the (online) tests you take be considered a complete or fully accurate psychological portrait.
Always go to a (mental) health professional for a sound advice and thorough diagnosis.

# Chapter 5 - What Causes Anxiety Disorders?

So is there one set thing that causes anxiety disorders?

When I was diagnosed a big thing for me was trying to find out what could have caused it. I felt I could understand my issue if I knew why it was happening to me. Was there a gene I was born with or a gene I was missing? Was it something I learned growing up? Or was it my body's way of telling me I was under too much stress?

I found out there is no easy simple reason for why people develop anxiety. In fact all the reasons I listed above could have contributed to my anxiety. It is a bit on the complicated side. There are several reasons why an anxiety disorder might be brought on. It could be heredity, biology, family background, recent stress levels, your personal beliefs and your ability to express feelings or chemical imbalances.

## *Long Term, Predisposing Causes*

Studies have shown that there are three major long-term predisposing factors playing a role in the cause of anxiety disorders. Cumulative stress over time, childhood circumstances and heredity factors.

### Heredity Factors

While studies have shown that 15 to 25% of children who have parents who suffer from agoraphobia wind up suffering from it themselves, doctors are quick to say that these numbers are because it can be a learned condition. Meaning that if a child witnesses his or her parent being afraid to step into an elevator, they might grow up with the same fear. However you can inherit a general personality type that can predispose you to be excessively anxious which can lead to an anxiety disorder.

I have a grandmother who suffers from anxiety, while I didn't inherit the anxiety disorder from her because it is a different kind. I more than likely inherited the gene that she might carry that makes me more prone to anxiety. We are the only two people in my family to suffer from anxiety; however both my mother and brother have stomach issues when they are faced with stressful situations. This isn't to say that everyone who has an anxiety disorder in his or her family will have one too.

### Childhood Circumstances

There are some things that can happen in your childhood that can put you at risk for developing anxiety. I'm not saying that everyone who might experience one of these circumstances develops a disorder, but they can be at an increased risk. Nor am I saying the parents are at fault here either. While I had some of the same circumstances growing up, it is unfair for me to blame my parents for my disorder.

Children who grow up in an environment that is overly cautious can be at risk because they tend to worry excessively and be too concerned with safety. Children who are criticized a lot and have a lot expected from them tend to become very self critical as adults and feel that they are never good enough. In fact children who have low self-esteem have a high risk of developing an anxiety disorder when they are older. They might grow up being afraid of being rejected or that people won't like them. So they create a persona of whom they "should" be and not what they are.

Living a life like this is stressful. No one is perfect, yet these children grow up believing that they should be. They never say no to anyone or anything even when they want to. Eventually the anxiety is the body's way of trying to tell them to take a break. This is one of the reasons why some therapists find it so important to talk about your childhood and resolve some of the unresolved issues that some people may have so they can move forward with their recovery. For me, it never worked and I always felt that what was in the past, should stay in the past. Other people may feel differently and benefit greatly from treatment like this.

## Cumulative Stress Over Time

Everyone has stress. There is just no way to avoid it. Morning traffic can cause stress, and your job can cause stress, sometimes just deciding what to make for dinner can cause stress. Stress is an everyday part of life. However when stress persists without a break it tends to build up. It is more just than your normal everyday stress. It could be problems with your relationship, your health or money that last for a number of years.

People living in Western society are experiencing more stress than they did at any previous time in history, and it is this stress that probably explains the increased occurrence of anxiety disorders. Anxiety can also be caused by going through many life events in a short amount of time.

There is a life events survey that many doctors use to gain an indication of the possible stress level you might have accumulated over a 2-year span. They list stressful situations and score each one. The highest being death of a spouse, the lowest being a minor violation of the law. You are to find out which of these events you have experienced within the 2-year period and then tally up your score. If you score under 150, you are less likely to be suffering from the effects of cumulative stress. A score from 151-300 means you could be suffering from chronic stress depending on how you handled the life event that took place and you might benefit from relaxation techniques. Anything over 300 means you are more than likely experiencing some harmful effects of the stress.

When I filled out this survey my score was well over 300! I had lost my father, my job, moved to a new place to live, had my mother get remarried, start a new relationship, start a new job, quit that job and started a new one, and moved in with someone all in the span of two years. Is it any wonder I was having panic attacks.

## Life Events Survey

- Death of spouse 100
- Divorce 73
- Marital separation 65
- Jail term 63
- Death of close family member 63
- Personal injury or illness 53
- Marriage 50
- Being fired from work 47
- Marital problems 45
- Retirement 45
- Change in health of family member 44
- Pregnancy 40
- Sexual difficulties 39
- Gain of new family member 39
- Business readjustment 39
- Change in finances 38
- Death of close friend 37
- Change to different line of work 36
- Change in number of arguments with spouse 35
- Mortgage or loan for major purchase such as a home 31
- Foreclosure of mortgage or loan 30
- Change in responsibilities at work 29
- Son or daughter leaving home 29
- Trouble with in-laws 29
- Outstanding personal achievement 28
- Beginning or finishing school 26
- Change in living conditions 25
- Revision of personal habits 24
- Trouble with boss 23
- Change in work hours or conditions 20
- Change in residence 20
- Change in school 20
- Change in recreation 19
- Change in church activities 19
- Change in social activities 18
- Mortgage or loan for lesser purchase (such as a car or tv) 17
- Change in sleeping habits 16
- Change in number of family get-together's 15
- Change in eating habits 15
- Vacation 13
- Christmas 12
- Minor violations of the law 11

Note: It has been shown that stress is accumulated over time. Having one major life event might raise your stress level (for example 50) but it takes possibly 12 months under normal conditions to reduce this to previous levels again. Many people don't realize that something else happening during this 'recovery' period will add to the level taking it even higher. The higher the level the more likely it is that you will experience negative or even physically damaging affects.

Even minor levels of stress suffered over a prolonged period can lead to stress related problems but higher levels can lead to physical ailments and more severe psychological disorders.

Many people do handle stress differently than others. There are some people out there who can let stress just roll off their backs and never get panicky at all. There are others who thrive on stress and it encourages them to do more.

Some people have so much stress in their lives that they can't handle it even if they tried. These are the people who are more prone to anxiety than other people. They cannot let the worries of their day go. It keeps them awake at night and they cannot focus on any other activities other than what is causing them the stress.

## Chemical Imbalances

A chemical imbalance can be the cause of a number of mental illnesses. Anxiety but also depression, ADHD and bipolar disorders. While no doctor is 100% sure what causes a chemical imbalance they have found that these common types of imbalances affect people's mental health.

- Availability of neurotransmitters like serotonin, dopamine, Norepinephrine, GABA and acetylcholine
- Increased levels of toxic neurochemicals
- Lower levels of Magnesium, Zinc, or Potassium
- Low Levels of vitamins like B6, B9, B12 (all stress reducing vitamins) and Vitamin-C
- Undersupply of key cofactors like amino acids that are used to help transport neurotransmitter forerunners into the blood-brain barrier.
- Increased cortisol hormone levels.

Lately in the medical profession, doctors seem quick to decide that a chemical imbalance is what causes anxiety disorders. So let's get back to the question of what causes a chemical imbalance.

Over the years several possible reasons have been given for the imbalance such as genetic factors or irregular brain development. Some researchers follow the theory that your own thoughts and actions can cause this imbalance. However it seems almost impossible to come up with conclusive evidence. But why are many doctors nevertheless inclined to say that you may have a chemical imbalance causing your anxiety disorder if they are not a hundred percent sure what it is? This could be credited to a number of reasons. Most likely it is because a chemical imbalance can be easily treated with medication. So besides the three long-term, predisposing causes there is also a fourth, a chemical imbalance, that can cause or help contribute to your anxiety disorder.

## Short-Term, Triggering Causes

Long term causes such as heredity, childhood environment, and cumulative stress create a predisposition to anxiety disorders. Yet it often takes more specific conditions, operating over a short period of time, to actually trigger panic attacks or cause a phobia to develop. Significant personal loss, significant life change, stimulants such as caffeine or nicotine, or the drugs marijuana or psilocybin, can act as triggers.

## Maintaining Causes

Maintaining causes of anxiety disorders can be several things. For instance avoidance of panic provoking situations or environments, anxious/negative self-talk ("what if thinking"), mistaken beliefs ("these symptoms are harmful and/or dangerous"), withheld feelings, lack of assertiveness. These behaviors impede your healing and stop you from enjoying an anxiety-free life.

Recognizing these barriers can be a great first step toward getting rid of your problems. For instance anxious/negative self-talk.

When you are obsessively negative, it means that you have a tendency toward being "negative" about people, places, situations, and things in your life. Perhaps you find yourself saying things like "I can't do this!" or "No one understands!" or "Nothing ever works!", for example. You may be doing this unconsciously, but essentially you have what's known as a "sour grapes" attitude, and it holds you back from knowing what it's like to view life from a positive lens and enjoy the beauty in yourself and people around you! There's a whole world out there for you...with happiness and positive thinking.

When you engage in obsessive perfectionism, you are centered on trying to do everything "just so" to the point of driving yourself into an anxious state of being. You may find yourself making statements such as, "I have to do this right, or I'll be a failure!" or "If I am not precise, people will be mad at me!" Again, this behavior may be under the threshold of your awareness, but it interferes greatly with your ability to enjoy things without feeling "uptight" and "stressed."

When you are obsessed about analyzing things, you find yourself wanting to rehash a task or an issue over and over again. For instance, you might find yourself making statements such as, "I need to look this over, study it, and know it inside and out...or else I can't relax!" or "If I relax and let things go without looking them over repeatedly, things go wrong!" While analytical thinking is an excellent trait, if it's done in excess you never get to stop and smell the roses because you're too busy trying to analyze everything and everyone around you.

Gaining insight into this behavior is one of the most important keys to letting go of stress, and getting complete power over your anxiety.

35

If you find yourself engaging in any of the above behaviors, there are two things you can do to help yourself. First, ask the people you know, love, and trust, "Am I negative about things?" "Do I complain a lot?" and "Am I difficult to be around?"

This may be hard for you to listen to, as the truth sometimes hurts a great deal. But the insight you will get from others' assessment of you is invaluable, and you'll know precisely how others see you. Accept their comments as helpful info, and know that you will gain amazing insights from what you hear.

Second, keep a journal to write down and establish patterns of when you are using "hurtful behaviors." Even if you are not thrilled with the idea of writing, you can make little entries into a notebook or journal each day. The great part is that you'll begin to see patterns in your behavior that reveal exactly what you're doing to prevent yourself from curing your anxiety.

Now what more can you do to treat your anxiety disorder?

# Chapter 6 - Anxiety Treatment

The choices of treatment include cognitive behavioral therapy, lifestyle changes, and/or pharmaceutical therapy (medications).

Mainstream treatment for anxiety consists of the prescription of anxiolytic agents and/or antidepressants and/or referral to a cognitive-behavioral therapist. Treatment controversy arises because some studies suggest that a combination of the medications and behavioral therapy can be more effective than either one alone.

In children, the World Health Organization says that cognitive behavioral therapy in the form of the Friends for Life Program is best practice to treat anxiety.

The right treatment may depend much on the individual's genetics and environmental factors. Therefore it is important to work closely with a psychiatrist, therapist or counselor who is familiar with anxiety disorders and current treatments.

Several drugs can be prescribed to treat these disorders. These include benzodiazepines (such as Xanax), antidepressants of most of the main classes (SSRI, TCAs, MAOIs), and possibly Quetiapine.

What helped me most was a combination of pills (briefly a tranquilizer followed by an antidepressant in combination with therapy). However there is no best cure fitting all. It's a personal journey to learn how to cope with anxiety or to beat it.

## Curing Panic Attacks
Most doctors will begin the process of curing your panic attacks by prescribing anti-anxiety medication. This will allow a few things to happen: Your physical symptoms will decrease or go away. Your mood and mental condition will stabilize. You will be able to live again without fearing the onset of a panic attack.

After you have gotten your feet back under you and the medications are working, your doctor will recommend a therapist. The role therapy plays in curing panic attacks cannot be underestimated. While the medications can provide relief from the symptoms, a true cure for your panic attacks can only come from within yourself. A therapist will help you work through the issues that are causing the panic attacks in the first place. It is very rare that a person has panic attacks without some underlying factor causing it. Only after these issues have been worked through will curing your panic attacks be complete.

## *Where To Get Help For Your Anxiety?*

If you have exhausted all your own mental power to overcome Anxiety on your own, there is still help for you.

The best course of action for you at this point is to seek out professional help through your trusted family physician. He will tell you what you should do and the best steps for you to take to have a fulfilling life with a dash of Anxiety on the side ;-). If you don't have a family physician, you can still get help for Anxiety through your local area mental health facilities.

Never think that you are going through this alone. There are millions of other people struggling with Anxiety just like you every single day. There are support groups, counseling services you should take advantage of, Anxiety related programs to help you make sense of and learn to control your Anxiety, and of course there are effective medicines your doctor can prescribe for you if necessary.

## *Choosing The Right Mental Health Professional*

You have several choices in selecting a mental health professional:
- psychiatrists
- psychologists
- clinical social workers
- other types of counselors

There are differences in the training and licensing requirements among these professions, and choosing among them can seem complicated. I don't want to complicate your job here, so I'm going to offer you some simple advice on selecting one.
Not everyone will agree with my advice, and you should assume it reflects my own biases.

Psychiatrists are doctors who specialize in mental health. They generally use medication as their treatment method, because that is their area of specialty. Because odds are high that a psychiatrist will recommend medication to you, and will probably be much less familiar with cognitive behavioral methods than other practitioners, I suggest you select one of the other professions for your first consultation. Of course, if you want medication, you should go directly to a psychiatrist.
Which other profession? I think this is less important than finding a professional who has some specialized training and experience with the cognitive behavioral treatment of panic. In major urban areas, such people are available, if you know how to look. In rural areas, unfortunately, there are often none.

## Medication

Medication can be very useful in treating anxiety disorders and is often used in combination with other forms of therapy, such as cognitive-behavioral therapy. The most important aspect of the process of beginning with medication is to have an open and honest discussion with your physician, followed by ongoing evaluation and monitoring.

Last year, there were some 40 million Americans treated for anxiety and panic disorders. If you are one of the many who are experiencing severe panic attacks on a regular basis, there are treatment options available that can reduce or eliminate the panic attacks. Don't let panic attacks rule your life any longer. Read on to learn about some of the panic attack medications available.

The most commonly prescribed panic attack medication is one of the various forms of antidepressants. These medications help to keep your anxiety and stress levels down to a manageable level. They also help with any depression conditions you may have, which is not uncommon in anxiety disorder patients. There is a chemical imbalance in your brain that is responsible for the magnified effects of everyday stresses. Two main neurotransmitters (serotonin and norepinephrine) are related to your mood, and these are the chemicals targeted by antidepressants. While most antidepressants work by correcting the levels of these neurotransmitters in your brain, how they go about it can be completely different from product to product.

The panic attack medications Zoloft, Paxil, and Prozac are all selective serotonin reuptake inhibitors. Xanax, Valium, Klonopin, and Ativan are all a class of antidepressant called benzodiazapines. Norpramin, Anafranil, and Tofranil are tricyclic antidepressants. Parnate and Nardil are both monomine oxidase inhibitors. These last two types are prescribed much more rarely nowadays than the first two classifications of antidepressant. Knowing what type of antidepressant you are currently taking is very important, as some other medications, even over-the-counter ones, can react badly with certain classes of antidepressant.

Always ask your doctor about any possible drug interactions. All of these panic attack medications, while usually quite effective, can have some unpleasant side effects. Usually these side effects are most pronounced if your dosage is too high, but they can occur at any dosage. The more common side effects of antidepressants include: dry mouth, constipation, dizziness, drowsiness, headaches, blurred vision, sexual problems, nausea, heart palpitations, racing heart, weight gain, nightmares, insomnia, and nervousness. While some of these side effects may be better than having panic attacks, if they are too much they can cause more stress than the medications can relieve.

If at any time you feel that the side effects are just too much, you should discuss changing your medication with your doctor. Remember, everyone is different. All medication do not affect everybody the same way. What works for one person may not work for you, and it can take time and effort to find the panic attack medications that work best for you. Your doctor may have to change your panic attack medication several times, but with so many different antidepressant and dosages available odds are good that you will find the medications that work for you. And once you have found the panic attack medications that best control your symptoms, don't stop taking them just because you are feeling better. The medicines just deal with the symptoms, they are not a final cure for your panic disorder.

Medications for social phobias anxiety are just one part of an overall treatment for this condition. Social phobias can sometimes be overcome when left untreated but most of the times they tend to become worse, hence therapy and medication are both important.

Therapy can enable people suffering from social phobias to cope with and overcome the phobia. To fight the symptoms, medications are often subscribed. The patients are also given exercises to build up their self esteem during therapies as this is crucial while tackling social phobias.

## Be Careful And Easy Does It
With more and more people every year suffering from some form of anxiety disorder, getting a prescription for one of the many anxiety medications that are out there can mean all the difference for many of them. But regardless of the specific medications used, there are some things you should take into account both before and during treatment.

Talk to Your Doctor. The first step is to go and talk to your doctor. He will likely have many questions to ask you as part of his diagnostic procedure. If he does diagnose you with an anxiety disorder, there are some things you should discuss before the prescription is written. If improperly prescribed or used, anxiety medications can be dangerous.

Some things you should be sure and talk to your doctor about include:
- Your full medical history: Your doctor should have a copy of your full medical history. If not, be sure and discuss anything that you have been diagnosed with or had prescribed already. Your family medical history and any medical conditions you have should also be brought up; certain anxiety medications can be dangerous to people with, say, a heart condition or a predisposition towards one.
- Any medications you are currently on: Provide a full list of everything you are taking to your doctor. Some anxiety medications can produce an adverse reaction in combination with other medications.
- Addiction issues: Be sure and tell your doctor if you have had trouble with addictions in the past. While this will not preclude you from taking anxiety medications, your doctor knows that the course of treatment should be more closely monitored for signs of dependency.

**Things to keep in mind during treatment**

Anxiety medications are fantastic for alleviating the symptoms of your anxiety disorder. But for the medication to have the most effect, there are some things to keep in mind.

- Take medication as prescribed: This is extremely important. Some anxiety medications are cyclic drugs, which means they take time to start working. Do not stop taking the medication because it doesn't appear to be working, and don't take more than prescribed in an attempt to cause an effect. Follow the dosage amounts carefully, and pay attention to any special instructions, such as "only with food" or "2 hours before eating".
- Report any side effects: If you experience any side effects, tell your doctor immediately. Some anxiety medications can cause serious side effects in some people. In some cases, emergency medical treatment may be required (such as a previously unknown allergic reaction).
- Discuss any new medications: Make sure that the prescribing doctor knows about any new medications that you are using. This includes herbal supplements and over-the-counter medications. It is better to be safe than sorry when mixing medicines.

When properly used, anxiety medications can provide the help a person needs to get through their anxiety disorder and on the road to recovery. But improperly using or abusing your anxiety medication can cause serious problems, and may worsen your condition in the long run. So follow directions, and keep in touch with your doctor.

## Benzodiazephines

When I was in the hospital I was given Xanax. Xanax is a high-potency benzodiazepine (BZs). Xanax and other drugs of this nature like Ativan and Klonopin slow down the central nervous system and decreases anxiety. It relaxes you. Xanax and other BZs work very quickly. Most people usually feel the symptoms subsiding after only 15-20 minutes. I used to tell myself if I could hold on for a half hour after taking a Xanax it would be all right. Another plus to this is that it can be taken on an as needed basis. You can take a small dose of it before you face a challenging situation. I'm claustrophobic so the first time I went for my MRI and MRA, I had to stop before they could even start because I was so scared. In case you never had one before, they insert your upper body into a tube like tunnel that is very small and tight. When I went back to try again, I took a Xanax to help reduce my fears and was able to make it through the whole procedure. There are also hardly any side effects for many people when compared to antidepressants. Although some people have reported feeling sleepy the day after taking the Xanax or experience headaches.

However, Xanax and other BZs are addictive, which is why they should be taken on an as needed only basis. The higher the dosage and the more you take it, the harder it will be to get off it. Withdrawal from these medications can be difficult although there have been some studies that show Klonopin has less severe withdrawal symptoms than Xanax. If you wean yourself off any BZs to quickly you might experience what is known as rebound anxiety but the symptoms will be greater than the ones you initially experienced. Most people should wean themselves off it slowly over a period of six months or so if they find they are addictive to it. If you are addictive to it, talk to your doctor to come up with a plan of action to wean yourself off it.

**Tip:**
Keep in mind that any decision about taking medication is highly personal. It should only be made in conjunction with your mental health professional. Ask about the types of prescriptions available, their effectiveness, dosages and side effects so you have a good understanding of what to expect.

Another disadvantage to BZs is that they are effective only while you are taking them. After you stop taking them there is a 100% chance your anxiety will return unless you have learned how to handle difficult situations and made some changes to help you achieve long-term anxiety relief.

In my experience with Xanax, I never had a problem with it becoming addictive because to deal with my attacks I worked on trying to find other ways without medications. There were a few times when I could not calm myself down enough to ride the attack out that I did need to take a Xanax but it was never a routine for me. In fact after the first few months or so, I barely touched the stuff. There are some people who can take Xanax and not become addictive to it and others who do become addictive to it and need their doctors help weaning from it.

**How do drugs for anxiety work?**
Chemical substances in the brain called neurotransmitters help messages pass from nerve to nerve. When a person is anxious, certain neurotransmitters become imbalanced and the brain becomes abnormally active. Drugs can be used to block or slow down this increased activity and thereby relieve the physical nature of the anxiety.
- Benzodiazepines.
  These increase the actions of a particular neurotransmitter in the brain called GABA, high levels of which slow down the overactive brain. One example is diazepam, better known as Valium.
- Buspirone.
  This scales down activity in the brain by decreasing the effects of the neurotransmitter serotonin. It has fewer side effects than the benzodiazepines, although it takes longer to work.
- Beta-blockers
  These drugs interfere with neurotransmitters in the brain, heart, and muscles to reduce the physical symptoms of anxiety such as palpitations and tremor. The most commonly used beta-blocker is propranolol.

What are the adverse effects? The main drawback of the benzodiazepines is that they can cause drowsiness, and in some people, dizziness and confusion, so they should only be used in the short term. Also, if these drugs are used for a long time, the dose can become ineffective and dependence may develop. Buspirone does not carry the risk of dependence, bur occasionally people experience dizziness, headaches, or stomach ulcers. Beta-blockers are generally well tolerated but can cause coldness of the fingers and toes, and sleep disturbances.

## SSRI Antidepressant Medications

Selective serotonin reuptake inhibitors or SSRI as they are commonly known contain some of the well-known antidepressants such as Prozac, Zoloft, Lexapro, Paxil, Luvox and Celexa. They are the first choice medications that are used by most doctors to treat anxiety disorders. As we said earlier, a cause of anxiety disorders could be a chemical imbalance caused by lack of neurotransmitters like serotonin.

SSRIs increase levels of serotonin in the brain by preventing the reabsorption of it in the spaces between the nerve cells. By doing that the number of serotonin receptors on the brain cells decrease and become less sensitive to changes in the neuro chemicals environment of the brain that is caused by stress. This usually takes about two months to take place which is why you won't feel an instant change when beginning one of these medications. SSRIs are used most often to treat panic, panic with agoraphobia and obsessive compulsive disorder. Occasionally they will be used to treat post traumatic stress disorder, especially if it is accompanied by depression. Usually a person on an SSRI will have to take it for 1 to 2 years to feel the full effect of it.

A common myth about antidepressants is that people become addictive on them, this is not true. They are not addictive. Another misconception is that they lead to weight gain, again this is not always true.

There are some drawbacks to using these medications. As with almost any medication there is always a risk of side effects and SSRIs are not different. Some of the common side effects are jitteriness, restlessness, dizziness, drowsiness, headaches, nausea and a decreased sexual drive. These usually go away within two weeks of starting the medication. Relapse is low with SSRIs when compared with BZs.

Another drawback is that it could take up to a month or more before people start seeing any real benefit from taking it. This is why sometimes your doctor might prescribe you a BZ like Xanax to help you get through the first month or so. The biggest complaint from people is that they did not get results from the medications fast enough so they went off them and their symptoms returned.

I was given the alternative of taking Lexapro but any medication without the Xanax was not an option for me. Medication has been a lifesaver for many people and has kept them sane, but again it is not for everyone.
SSRI type medication functions by stopping serotonin, a neurotransmitter from getting reabsorbed into particular cells of the brain. This ends up leaving a larger amount of serotonin in the brain. Issues with serotonin are connected to depression and anxiety disorders.

43

There are many brand names for SSRIs. Medications for social phobias anxiety such as Zoloft and Prozac are SSRIs

## Tricyclic Antidepressants

These antidepressants included Tofranil, Pamelor, Norpramin, Anafranil and Sinequian among others. They are commonly used to treat panic attacks. They reduce both the frequency and intensity of the panic attacks in people. They can also help reduce depression that sometimes comes with panic attacks. Anafranil seem to be helpful in treating OCD.

The problem is Tricyclics have worse side effects than say the SSRIs. In fact they are not used that much at all when compared to SSRIs. There were studies done of imipramine and one third of the subjects had to drop out because they could not tolerate the side effects. The side effects included dry mouth, blurred vision, dizziness that can be caused by hypertension, weight gain, and sexual dysfunction can occur. Some people complain that anxiety can actually increase the first few days of taking this drug. The problem is that even though most of these side effects do go away after the first week or so, there were still 25% to 30% of people who continue to have the side effect even after the first few weeks. Also, almost half of the people who use these antidepressants relapse after stopping use of this drug.

## MAO-Inhibitor Antidepressants

If you have tried everything else and found no relief, your doctor may try this class of antidepressant. MAO-Inhibitors are the oldest class of medications and Nardil is the most common one used for panic. These are effective antidepressants but usually used last because of the risks they contain. They can cause a serious and sometimes fatal rise in blood pressure when they are combined with certain foods, cheeses and wine and some over-the-counter medications. They do have a potent panic-blocking effect and are usually effective when all other options fail but some doctors feel that the side effects are not worth it. Besides common side effects like weight gain, low blood pressure, sexual dysfunction, headaches, fatigue and tiredness.

Dietary restrictions are very important when you are on MAO-Inhibitors. You have to take extra caution to avoid any foods with tyramine which means that most cheeses are out, homemade yogurts, alcoholic, aged meats, fish, bananas, and some vegetables. You also have to stop taking over-the-counter cold medicines and antihistamines.

MAOIs function by inhibiting some chemical activity in our brains. MAOIs medication for social phobias anxiety prevents the breaking down of a chemical called monoamine, again leaving more of the chemical in the brain. This type of medication for social phobias anxiety is used for curing social phobias disorders, depression and many other types of mental health concerns. There are many numbers of names for MAOI drugs such as Nardil, Aurorix and Marplan.

## Many Options

As you can see there are many options when it comes to taking medications, but how do you know if medications are for you. First, talk with your doctor to express any concerns you may have. You should consider these personal factors also; the severity of your problem, your personal feeling on taking medications, and your patience. As I have stated, you might not benefit from the medications for some time. Will you be able to wait that long for some relief?

Next you should look at how long you are going to be willing to take the medication. It is hard to say how long you will need to take it. Usually it depends on some factors. You should find out what type of medication you will be taking. BZs and some beta-blockers should be used on an "as needed" basis. While antidepressants are usually recommended for at least six months, most people stay on them for anywhere from 1 to 2 years if not longer. Some people might even decide to stay on them for longer than that on a lower dosage.

Also consider what type of anxiety you have. If your anxiety is mild you might only need to take the medication for a short time while you learn ways to deal with your anxiety natural. Other people who are having frequent panic attacks will probably need to take their medication for a longer time. If you suffer from OCD, a long-term use of an SSRI medication is usually recommended. Usually about 2 years or more before the dosage could be lowered to see what dosage might work best for you to correct the neurobiological problem that accompanies OCD. The more severe the disorder, the longer you should stay on the medication. You also need to see if you can eliminate or at least reduce your need for medication at least in the long run. If you follow a program of natural approaches and stick with it, your brain can recover. You just have to be motivated and committed to the natural approaches that we will touch on later.

When you decide to stop relying on medication there are some guidelines you should keep in mind before you stop.
The first one is to make sure you have gained experience with the basic strategies for overcoming anxiety and panic. For example, if you have established a daily practice of deep relaxation and exercise.
Secondly, make sure you talk to your doctor to see if he wants to set up a program for you to taper off the drugs especially if you are stopping any BZ.
Next, be prepared to depend on more natural techniques to get through the panic attacks and last do not be disappointed if you need to rely on the medication again for periods of anxiety and stress. You might find that short-term use of the medication you stopped using might be helpful during certain times of the year especially if you are like me.

My panic disorder tends to intensify during the winter months and although I haven't taken Xanax in almost 3 years, I make sure to keep some just in case. Medication is not for everyone and if it does not work for you, do not feel like a failure. There are plenty of other options when dealing with anxiety disorders.

## Natural Supplements

If you are a little weary of taking prescribed medications, you might find some benefit in taking a natural supplement. There are many supplements that are available at your local drugstore. Most people find supplements beneficial if their condition is not out of control but more of a nuisance in their life.

While you may not believe it, using natural remedies for panic attacks can be just as effective as a prescription medication. These natural remedies are often better for you as well, with fewer or no side effects. Contrast this with prescription anxiety medications, which can cause all sorts of unpleasant side effects; some of the side effects commonly experienced are: heart palpitations, racing heart, dry mouth, sexual problems, constipation, and drowsiness. These are just the more common side effects. Also, in some individuals, these prescriptions can have the opposite effect they are supposed to have, increasing anxiety instead of decreasing it. Using natural remedies can avoid these unpleasant side effects. It is entirely possible to feel calmer and have fewer panic attacks using these natural remedies. Unlike prescription medications, however, natural remedies are usually not approved by the FDA for the treatment of any condition. Just be aware of your own reactions to a natural remedy and stop using it if you experience any side effects that bother you.

Kava is one of the most recommended anti anxiety supplements. It is usually found in the pacific. Most people who have used kava report that they feel relaxation minus the drugged feeling, a sense of peacefulness, they find that they are more sociable and initially feel an alertness that can be followed a few hours later by drowsiness so it is ok to take in the evening. The one thing to remember about Kava is that it cannot be taken every day. It should only be taken no more than three times a week and you should always give yourself one week off the Kava. The most common side effects are tiredness and decreased sex drive.

A few of the natural remedies available for panic attacks are lemon balm, lavender, and passiflora. These herbs are said to be highly effective in the treatment of panic attacks and for general stress and anxiety relief. Most often these are available in products with other ingredients that enhance their relaxing effect. There is a particular brand of herbal mixture called Pure Calm. This product contains all three of the above ingredients, and is very effective at relieving stress and anxiety, reducing the number of panic attacks you experience.

Another name brand herbal remedy is called Panicyl. This product contains ginseng, ashwaganda, Rhodiala Rosea, and a mixture of various amino acids that work together to relax and enhance your mood by balancing neurotransmitter levels in your brain. This acts to reduce your anxiety and help with depression, which reduces the frequency and severity of your panic attacks.

Another common natural supplement is St. Johns Wort. St. Johns Wort or Hypericium as it is sometimes also referred to has been said to be nature's Prozac. This herb is usually taken in capsule form to provide many of the same benefits as Panicyl, and has been proven to significantly reduce the frequency of panic attacks if taken regularly. There are some side effect with St. John's Wort. Some people become more sensitive to the sun; have headaches, dizziness, dry mouth and constipation. Another thing to keep in mind is that you should not take St. Johns Wort if you are on oral birth control pills. Studies have shown that St. John's Wort decreases the effectiveness of the pill.

Some of these products should not be taken with certain prescription medications, as they may produce an adverse reaction or interfere with the effectiveness of the medication. Always talk with your doctor before starting on any homeopathic treatment plans.

When taken regularly, natural remedies for panic attacks have been shown to be as effective in some cases as prescription medications, but with a far lower occurrence of side effects. They are all available over-the-counter, and are usually reasonably priced. You can start taking them immediately. But if you are on other medication, always talk to your doctor before taking any of these natural remedies for panic attacks.

Many of these supplements such as Kava and St. John Wort along with several others like Passion Flower, and Valerian are used more than prescribed antidepressants because most people report feeling the better after a week or so on the natural supplements vs. a few weeks or more on the prescribed medication.

**Tip:**
If you are pregnant or have health problems, check with your doctor before taking herbs. There is however one supplement that is very different from St. Johns Wort and Kava and that is SAM-e (S-adenosyl-methionine). SAM-e differs from them and other herbs that are used for depression because it occurs naturally in our bodies. SAM-e increases serotonin and dopamine activity in the brain. Some doctors believe that people who are lacking enough SAM-e in their bodies are usually clinically depressed or suffer from anxiety. Another pro with SAM-e is there are almost no side effects aside for some queasiness the first few days of taking it. SAM-e also works fast. Most people will feel better within a few days of taking it. Not only does it help with depression and anxiety but it also helps with joint pain and liver function.

**Warnings:**
Individuals using prescribed medication such as antidepressant, including Serotonin Re-Uptake Inhibitors and MAO Inhibitors should consult a doctor before using. Individuals with Parkinson's disease, bi-polar disorder or manic depression should not use SAM-e. To be sure if SAM-e is safe to use consult your doctor. Medications will work best for people who are suffering from OCD and PTSD but those who suffer from panic disorders might find it more helpful to rely on other methods to manage their panic instead of medication. There is

no set cure for panic attacks, but learning how to manage them will help decrease the occurrence.

Read on to find out how to manage your panic and anxiety using therapy.

## *Therapy*

There are several treatments that have proven to be most successful in treating the various Anxiety Disorders. I have listed the several treatment options along side with the disorders that are most regularly treated with them. This list however can not be leading in the treatment. You should always find out what suits you best in dialogue with a (mental) health care professional.

### Combination Therapy

In many cases it would appear that the ideal treatment for anxiety disorders is a combination of medication and therapy.
You might find this list helpful to find your way to the right therapist.

### Panic Attacks
- Relaxation Training
- Medication
- Lifestyle and Personality Changes
- Panic-Control Therapy
- Interoceptive Desensitization

### Agoraphobia
- Relaxation Training
- Cognitive Therapy
- Medication
- Exposure
- Assertiveness Training
- Group Therapy

### Social Phobia
- Relaxation Training
- Cognitive Therapy
- Medication
- Exposure
- Assertiveness Training
- Staying on task
- Social Skills Training

### Specific Phobia
- Relaxation Training
- Cognitive Therapy
- Exposure

### GAD = Generalized Anxiety Disorder
- Relaxation Training

- Cognitive Therapy
- Worry Exposure
- Reducing Worry Behaviors
- Problem Solving
- Distraction
- Mindfulness Practice

## OCD = Obsessive Compulsory Disorders
- Relaxation Training
- Cognitive Therapy
- Medication
- Exposure
- Lifestyle and Personality Changes
- Exposure and Response Prevention

## PTSD = Post Traumatic Stress Disorder
- Relaxation Training
- Cognitive Therapy
- Medication
- Exposure
- Support Groups
- EMDR or Hypnotherapy

## Relaxation Training

Practicing abdominal breathing and some form of deep muscle relaxation techniques (such as progressive muscle relaxation) on a daily basis. This helps to reduce the physical symptoms of panic as well as anticipatory anxiety you might experience about having a panic attack. It also helps to better control anxiety symptoms.

## Cognitive Behavioral Therapy

### Tip:
Always ask about cognitive-behavioral therapy. Experience has shown this therapy is one of the most effective and long-lasting treatments available for people with anxiety disorders. A Cognitive Behavioral Therapy (CBT) is a psychotherapy based on changing cognitions, assumptions, beliefs and behaviors, with the aim of influencing disturbed emotions. The general approach developed out of Cognitive Therapy has become widely used to treat various anxiety disorders. The particular therapeutic techniques vary according to the particular client or issue, but commonly include keeping a diary of significant events and associated feelings, thoughts and behaviors; questioning and testing cognitions, assumptions, evaluations and beliefs that might be unhelpful and unrealistic; gradually facing activities which may have been avoided; and trying out new ways of behaving and reacting. Basically, cognitive behavior works with the brain and how and what we think. It teaches us new ways of thinking and how to behave.

There is strong evidence that behaviorally based treatments are effective in treating at least some anxiety disorders. The aim of cognitive therapy is to help you replace exaggerated, fear thinking about panic and phobias with more realistic and supportive mental habits. When you worry, you overestimate the odds of something negative happening and underestimate your ability to cope if something bad did, in fact, happen. While insight is very much involved in this process, it is not insight into deep psychological causes, as in psychoanalysis, but, rather, practical commonsense problem solving. Some examples will illustrate the process:

- You learn to identify, challenge, and replace counterproductive thoughts with helpful ones.
- Fearful thoughts that perpetuate social phobias are identified, challenged, and replaced with more realistic thoughts. For example, the thought "I'll make a fool of myself if I speak up" would be replaced with the idea "It's okay if I'm a bit awkward at first when I speak up-most people won't be bothered."
- Fearful thoughts that tend to perpetuate the specific phobia are challenged and replaced. For example, "What if I panic because I feel trapped aboard an airplane?" would be replaced with more realistic and supportive thoughts, such as, "While I may not be able to leave the airplane for two hours, I can move around, such as leaving my seat to go to the bathroom several times if needed. If I start to feel panicky, I have many strategies for coping that I can use, including abdominal breathing, talking to my companion, listening to a relaxing tape, or taking medication, if necessary."
- Coping statements, such as, "I've handled this before and I can handle it again" or "This is just a thought; it has no validity," are also useful. These supportive coping statements are rehearsed until they are internalized.
- Fearful, superstitious, or guilty thoughts associated with obsessions are identified, challenged, and replaced. For example, the idea "If I have a thought of doing harm to my child, I might act on it" is replaced with "The thought of doing harm is just 'random noise' caused by the OCD. It has no significance. Just having the thought doesn't mean I'll do it."
- Fearful or depressed thinking is identified, challenged, and replaced with more productive thinking. For example, guilt about having been responsible for the trauma. Or having survived when someone you loved did not, would be challenged. You would reinforce yourself with supportive, constructive thoughts, such as, "What happened was horrible, and I accept that there is nothing I could have done to prevent it. I'm learning now that I can go on."

Cognitive behavioral therapy is not an overnight process. Even after patients have learned to recognize when and where their mental processes go awry, it can take months of effort to replace any dysfunctional cognitive-affective-behavioral processes or habit with a more reasonable, salutary one.

# Friends For Life Program

Friends for Life helps children and teenagers cope with feelings of fear, worry, and depression by building resilience and self-esteem and teaching cognitive and emotional skills in a simple, well-structured format.

Used in schools and clinics throughout the world, FRIENDS is the only childhood anxiety prevention program acknowledged by the World Health Organization for its 8 years of comprehensive evaluation and practice. It has proved effective for up to 6 years after initial exposure. The program is currently used in schools and clinics throughout Australia, New Zealand, Canada, the United Kingdom, Germany, the Netherlands, the United States, Mexico, Norway, and Portugal. FRIENDS is run by a school's own teachers and does not involve any clinical assessment or diagnosis, thus avoiding labeling children as anxious or different. Before starting a FRIENDS program, teachers attend a one-day group training workshop. These workshops are conducted regularly across Australia by Pathways Health and Research Centre and overseas by accredited training partners.

Anxiety is the most common form of mental disorder, affecting up to 15% of children and teenagers. Anxiety significantly interferes with a child's ability to confidently handle everyday situations, including relationships with peers, adults and family, and school achievement. If left unattended, anxiety difficulties may continue into young adulthood, sometimes leading to depression. FRIENDS combats anxiety by fostering an emotional resilience in children and teenagers that will stay with them for life. Completing a 10-session FRIENDS program can reduce a child's risk of developing a disorder for up to six years. Children with normal levels of worry benefit by acquiring resilience to emotional stress. FRIENDS promotes important personal development concepts such as self-esteem, problem-solving, self-expression, and building positive relationships with peers and adults, and therefore fits in well with the normal curriculum.

## Helping Your Child Overcome Fear

Does your child suffer the detrimental effects of fear? Fear is part of our emotional makeup that helps us to identify danger. When children sense that something is wrong, they may feel an intense anxiety, causing their heart rate and blood pressure to increase, as well as sweating, shaking or running away from their object of fear. In cases where children are highly fearful, they may run to their parents with loud shrieks or screams. The sense of fear may not relate proportionally to the threat or danger that is evident. This is called "irrational fear".

How do fears develop? There are several ways that children develop fear.
The child's first main contact with fear is usually developed by relating cause and effect. For instance, a loud noise like the discharge of a gun may cause a child to be afraid if they see negative effects resulting from the discharge. A child may run away to hide whenever they see a gun – avoiding the object of fear.

A second way that fear is developed in children is by observing the actions of others - usually their parents - and imitating them. For example, whenever a child sees a parent shriek or run away from a spider, the child learns that spiders are objects of fear.

Sometimes fears are developed when parents "reward" the child for showing a fearful response. For example, a child may avoid using a bath towel that has "germs" on it for fear of being contaminated. If a clean towel is given each time a child requests it because of "germs" then you are really only rewarding the fear response, rather than helping to solve the root cause.

How can parents help their child overcome fear? Here are seven steps to help your child overcome fear:

- Don't model fearful reactions
- Show them that you can handle difficult situations and don't need to avoid fearful situations
- Teach your child how to cope with fearful situations
- Praise your child when they cope rather than run away
- Keep a calm atmosphere during unsettled periods
- Stay firm and keep a positive outlook
- Talk about genuine threats to provide a balanced view

Your children's fear can be reduced by working through the fearful situation directly with your child. By showing that you are able to handle fearful situations you can help your child to "outgrow" most fears that are common in children.

## Exposure

Exposure therapy is suggested to be one of the best ways to overcome your anxiety.

To master something in life it is necessary first to think about it, and then practice doing it. Remember when you first started to learn how to drive. The more you practiced the better you became. This is the basis of exposure therapy. You need to go into the situation and think about it in a different way, implement the other skills and knowledge you have to manage your anxiety, and then reflect on how it went.

There is a word of caution here. Some research suggests to 'face the fear and do it anyway'. For some people this may work, however for others it doesn't. Learning the skills and techniques of cognitive therapy and educating yourself on where your anxiety is coming from in the first place, before exposing yourself to the situation, can often have better outcomes as you can feel more in control before you enter the situation, rather than going in feeling terrified.

When you feel anxious, it is suggested that you go through it first in your mind (realistic thinking/skills of cognitive therapy), and second, put yourself in the situation that you fear. This part is called exposure therapy.

For example, if you feared driving far from home, you would gradually increase the distance you drive in small increments. A support person might go with you in the same car, then drive in a second car behind you, and then, finally, you would practice driving alone. Or, if you were fearful of being home alone, the person who usually stays with you would leave for a few minutes at first and then gradually increase the time away. Over time you learn to confront, and enter into all of the situations you have been avoiding.

Another example in case of a social phobia could involve gradually and incrementally facing the social situation or situations you're phobic about. You might do this first imaginary and then in real life. For example, if you're phobic of public speaking, you might start out giving a one-minute talk to a friend and then gradually increase, through many steps, both the duration of what you say and the number of people you speak to. Or, if you have difficulty speaking up in groups, you'd gradually increase both the length and degree of self-disclosure of remarks made in a group setting. After each exposure, you'd review and challenge any unrealistic thinking that caused anxiety.

While the treatment for social phobia can be done on an individual basis, group therapy is the ideal treatment format. This allows direct exposure to the situation and stimuli that evoke anxiety in the first place.

Fear of flying would be faced first in imagination only, then by watching planes land and take off, then by boarding a grounded plane, then by taking a short flight, and, finally, a longer flight. A support person would accompany you first through all the steps, then you'd try them on your own.

For some phobias, it's difficult to do real-life exposure. For example, if you're afraid of earthquakes, treatment would emphasize cognitive therapy and then exposure to imagined scenes of earthquakes (or watching movies about earthquakes).

## Lifestyle Changes

Some of the lifestyle changes that can reduce your tendency to have panic attacks include stress management, regular exercise, removing stimulants and sugar from your diet, slowing down and creating "downtime," and changing attitudes toward perfectionism, an excessive need to please others, or the excessive need to control. Some examples include:

- Learn To Relax: Find a relaxation technique that works for you and use it to combat stress. Use breathing techniques to manage attacks.
- Exercise: It doesn't have to be anything too strenuous, just get out there and take a walk, go for a swim, or do something to develop a regular exercise routine. Studies have shown that exercise has a positive effect on mental health.
- Get Plenty Of Sleep: This is important for maintaining health and for keeping stress levels down.
- Talk With A Friend: Talking about what is bothering you can help relieve stress.

- Practice Good Time Management: Good planning can remove needless worry and running around which in turn will help reduce stress.
- Remove Stressful Activities From Your Life: Identify what causes you stress and remove it from your lifestyle when possible.
- Watch Your Diet: Eat food high in calcium, magnesium, phosphorus, and potassium since these nutrients are depleted by stress. Limit meats and other animal proteins and eat lots of fruits, grains, and vegetables instead.
- Avoid Caffeine: Caffeine can trigger panic attacks so avoid coffee, chocolate, some sodas and some teas, and other products containing caffeine.
- Avoid Refined Sugars And Simple Carbohydrates: Cut simple sugars, carbonated soft drinks and alcohol out of the diet

Studies showed that those who made these lifestyle changes experienced less panic and anxiety in one month and needed less doctor treatments than did those who did not make lifestyle changes! So take this advice seriously!

## Assertiveness training

Since agoraphobics often have difficulty standing up for themselves and their rights, and lack the ability to ask directly for what they want or to say no to what they don't want. Assertiveness training, a behavior therapy in which people are taught fitting methods of asserting themselves in various situations through honest and direct expression of their feelings, is often part of the treatment.

## Panic Control Therapy

The general goal of PCT is to foster within patients the ability to identify and correct maladaptive thoughts (such as, "I'm trapped!", 'I'm going to go crazy!" or "I'm going to have a heart attack!") and behaviors that launch, sustain, or worsen anxiety and panic attacks. In service of that goal, the treatment combines education, cognitive interventions, relaxation and controlled breathing procedures, and exposure techniques.

## Interoceptive Desensitization

Practicing voluntary habituation to the bodily symptoms of panic, such as rapid heartbeat, sweaty hands, shortness of breath, or dizziness. Such symptoms are created deliberately, usually in the therapist's office. For example, dizziness might be induced by spinning in a chair or rapid heartbeat by running up and down stairs. Repeated exposure to unpleasant bodily symptoms promotes desensitization, which means getting used to them so they no longer frighten you.

## Group Therapy

Group Psychotherapy is a form of psychotherapy during which one or several therapists treat a small group of clients together as a group. This may be more cost effective than individual therapy, and possibly even more productive.

Treatment for agoraphobia can be done effectively in a group setting. There is much support available in a group, both for realizing that you are not alone and for completing week-to-week homework assignments.

## Staying On Task

People with social phobia focus a lot on how they are doing or try to gauge other people's reactions while speaking in a social situation. Treatment includes training yourself to focus only on the task at hand, whether conversing with a boss, speaking up in class, or presenting information to a group.

## Social Skills Training

Social skills training (SST) is a form of behavior therapy used by teachers, therapists, and trainers to help anyone having difficulties relating to other people. Sometimes, learning basic social skills such as smiling and making eye contact, maintaining a conversation, self-disclosure, and active listening are part of the treatment for social phobia.

## Worry Exposure

Worry exposure requires that you do repeated and prolonged exposure to fearful images (your worst-case scenarios) of what you're worried about. This helps you become used to the worry, and helps you experience that worrying and anxiety do not cause negative events. In these images you include strategies you would use to reduce anxiety and cope with the situation.

## Reducing Worry Behaviors

You identify overly cautious "safety behaviors" that reinforce worrying. Pick the easiest behavior to stop and predict results of stopping it. For example, if you call your spouse or child several times a day to check on them, you would reduce the frequency of this behavior.

## Problem Solving

This means taking systematic action to solve the problem you're worried about. Focus on solutions to the problem that worries you instead of the worry itself. If there is no practical solution, you work on changing your attitude toward the situation, that is, learning to accept what you can't change.

## Distraction

Use distraction to change your thoughts or despair to thoughts of relaxation. Remember, the more desperate one is to relax, the more difficult relaxation can be. Luckily there are various distraction techniques that can be helpful for worries that do not lend themselves easily to cognitive therapy or problem solving. Common diversionary activities include talking to a friend, journaling, listening to music, gardening, exercise, puzzle solving, arts and crafts, cooking, and the Internet.

**Tip:**

Use humor whenever you can. Laughing is a great way to release stress. I bought the Fawlty Towers DVD box, a classic British sitcom from the 1970s set in a slightly crazy hotel, representing the height of the golden era of television comedy. Because it makes me laugh, again and again.

## Mindfulness Practice

Mindfulness is an attitude of simply witnessing the endless stream of your thoughts and feelings in the present moment without judgment. It originated in Buddhist meditation practice but is now being used as a common treatment for stress, depression, and generalized, anxiety.

## Exposure And Response Prevention (ERP)

This technique consists of exposure to situations that aggravate obsessions, followed by enforced prevention from performing rituals or compulsions. For example, if you've been washing your hands every time you touch a doorknob, you'd be taught to touch doorknobs and either reduce the number of times you wash your hands or refrain from washing at all. Similarly, if you check the door five times whenever you leave your house, you would be required to gradually reduce the number of checks to one.

You and your therapist devise various situations, preferably in your home setting. Then you continually practice exposing yourself to these situations and give up on performing the compulsions (response prevention). Usually your therapist or a support person accompanies you to check your compliance in not performing compulsions.

When your problem involves obsessions only, without compulsions, any neutralizing thoughts or covert rituals you use to reduce anxiety caused by your obsessions need to be stopped.

You would also work on accepting your obsessions without trying to make them go away.

## Support Groups

In a support group, members provide one another with various types of nonprofessional, nonmaterial help for a particular shared burdensome characteristic. The help may take the form of providing relevant information, relating personal experiences, listening to others' experiences, providing sympathetic understanding and setting up social networks. Support groups are helpful in enabling PTSD victims to realize that they are not alone. Support groups for rape or crime survivors are often available in larger metropolitan areas.

### EMDR Or Hypnotherapy

Eye-movement desensitization and reprocessing (EMDR) or hypnotherapy are often helpful in enabling PTSD victims to retrieve and work through memories of the original traumatic incident. These techniques may be used to speed up the course of therapy and/or overcome resistance to exposure.

## Affirmations

Besides therapy and medication there are some things you can do yourself that might give you that extra push forward. I developed personal affirmations and positive statements about the progress I was making, no matter how great or how small. These were often related to my panic attacks but sometimes also about life in general. You can always counter your negative thoughts with positive affirmations. These positive affirmations can build confidence and change negative behavior patterns into positive ones. The key is to base your affirmations on a rational assessment of fact and use them to fight against the negative thinking that might have undermined your self-confidence.

Here are some handy positive affirmations you might consider using.

- ✓ I can achieve my goals
- ✓ I can do this
- ✓ I am completely self-confident in every social situation
- ✓ I am completely myself, and people will like me
- ✓ I am in control of my life
- ✓ I am a valued person

Using positive affirmations can give you surprising strength but it isn't a cure for all ills. Decide rationally what goals you can realistically reach with hard work. Use positive thinking to reinforce these goals.

# Chapter 7 - Tips For A Support Person

My advice to people who care and would like to help somebody suffering from panic attacks would be to learn as much as you can about panic disorder. Then also know that you will probably have only about a 75% understanding of the panic anxiety. Ask the person with panic disorder to share how they feel, not during a panic attack, but rather when things are calm. Then find out what a panic attack is like for them.

- Just listen, don't try to solve the panic. As much as you, may want to, you can't fix it or take away the panic.
- Learn how you can support a person with panic disorder during an attack. It may mean just being there or giving them a hug. Those things can be more supportive than you may ever know.
- Let the person with panic disorder organize some activities that you can do together. You'll be surprised at how much they're willing to try if they can set their own parameters.
- Acknowledge those times when a panic sufferer sincerely says that they want to try to move forward or try activities despite their panic. Your support in this success can encourage them to try again.
- Compromise when possible. Be open to an adjustment that can easily be done that will make the outing successful and more comfortable. Change a departure time to avoid rush hour, take stairs instead of an elevator, and make adjustments for other, similar activities that are uncomfortable for the person with anxieties.
- Cancel plans under certain circumstances, if necessary. When you do make the decision to cancel, accept that decision and do it without guilt or accusations.
- Share your feelings as a support person. Good two-way communication can go a long way toward helping you both through the tough times.
- Work on keeping your relationship focused on the person you know and love. Understand that they are going through tough times, and care for them as you would in any other circumstance when they would need your help.
- Seek your own professional counseling. Living with someone with any type of disorder is going to bring up your own emotions and issues. Encourage the person with panic disorder to participate in a program for graduated exposure therapy. Offer to help them as a buddy to lean on during the initial and tough stages.
- Be a buddy or safe person. Be willing to be gentle and yet a bit firm. Encourage and comfort while helping the person focus on the task at hand. This is a specific role and may not be for everyone.

## What Can You Do To Support Someone?

As we go through this information, I want you to understand that this section is of importance to those trying to help another person who is experiencing, or dealing with anxiety on a daily basis. How you provide support to them may help them to control their Anxiety to some degree.

First thing is first. Never belittle or try to downplay someone's Anxiety Disorder. This is a real disorder and should be respected as such. Don't just dismiss their episode as a one-time event, or try and 'solve' their problem through rationalization.

You have to understand that when a person is actually going through an Anxiety attack rationality is not something they are concentrating on. Or listening to. This is an extremely frightening experience and no matter how much you'd want to, you cannot make this experience go away. Only the individual who is having the attack has the power to do this. Not you.

The absolute worst thing you can do is to act as if they are lying or acting to get attention. This is simply not the case. While you may believe this to be true because you have never yourself experienced the unrelenting terror of an anxiety attack, that doesn't mean that it isn't happening to someone you care about. Imagine for a second that you had witnessed a "physical" accident that your loved one or dear friend was a part of. Something you could see the outcome of. Wouldn't you do everything in your power to help them? What if they were trapped inside a car that was on fire? What if they were trapped underwater and were drowning? You would want to aid them, wouldn't you? What if they had stopped breathing? Would you just stand around watching them pass away? Or would you do everything you could to administer CPR to them, even if you weren't sure you were doing it correctly?

While the above examples are extreme, sometimes, to an Anxiety sufferer, it absolutely feels like the end of their world. As if they are drowning in a sea of chaos and disparity, unable to pull themselves out. Also, by attempting to in effect ignore the Anxiety attack, you are probably contributing to another disorder that goes hand in hand with anxiety. . .depression.

Instead of holding them down 'under water', try throwing them a life preserver the next time they have an attack. How can you do that? Just be there for them. Let them know that while you may not understand what they are going through, you are there for them and will stay until they feel better. Do not try and force someone out of an Anxiety attack. It could make the attack that much worse for them. Just let the attack happen naturally, and in most, if not all, cases, their bodies will help them come out of the 'hot' zone all on it's own. And if it doesn't, get them to the nearest emergency room as soon as you can. Or call an emergency squad to take them.

Also, never try and give someone suffering from an anxiety attack any type of prescription drugs that have not been prescribed by their family physician. Seems like common sense, but when you see a loved one going through such a painful event, you really want to help them. believe me, this will not help them. Getting them to a professional source, such as an emergency room or their own family physician for help, will.

# Chapter 8 - Nutrition And Anxiety

We've been spending much time talking about medications or herbs that can help with anxiety disorders, but let's take some time now to look at some lifestyle changes you can make to help you deal with anxiety disorders.

Can a good diet help your anxiety disorder?
According to research done for the past twenty years, the answer is yes. It has been shown that certain foods can create more stress and anxiety and others can create a sense of calmness. For years nutritionists have been trying to tell us that what we put in our bodies food wise, can have a direct effect on our emotions and it is about time that we start to listen to them.

**Tip:**
Don't skip meals, especially breakfast. Make sure you eat three healthy meals each day.

## Caffeine

The first thing you should look at is if you are taking in too much caffeine. Caffeine is famous for triggering panic attack. In fact the more coffee I drank, the worse my attacks were. I was a sodaholic. I could drink a 2 liter bottle of soda in a matter of hours regardless of the time. It wasn't until I started trying to learn other ways to control my panic attacks that I cut back on caffeine and when I became pregnant with my first child, I cut down even more and became so sensitive to caffeine that if I had even one glass of tea or soda with caffeine after 3pm. I was up all night. This is because caffeine increases the levels of neurotransmitters in your brain and that can cause you to feel alert and awake. It can also produce the same response as when you are faced with stress and that is a release of adrenaline. Caffeine can keep some people in a state of tension. How many times have you heard someone say about someone who is jumpy and jittery that they should "lay off the caffeine". While this is only an expression, it is a true statement about some people.

Now you might be reading this saying that you never drink coffee so this does not refer to you, but caffeine is not just in coffee. You can find caffeine in tea, sodas, chocolate candy, cocoa and many over-the-counter drugs like Excedrin. Also, do not let the words Decaffeinated fool you. Did you know that decaffeinated coffee contains 4 milligrams a cup? That might not seem a lot but think about how many cups you drink and add it up. Out of all the sodas Coca-Cola has the most amount of caffeine, almost as much as a cup of instant coffee, Cola has 65 mg while instant coffee has 66 mg. If you drink a lot of caffeine, it is recommended that you limit your caffeine intake to 100 mg a day. Use the figures below to figure out how much caffeine you consume in a day.

Instant Coffee- 66 mg
Coffee Drip- 146 mg
Teabag- 5 minute brew- 46 mg

Teabag- 1 minute brew- 28 mg
Cocoa- 13 mg
Coca-Cola- 65 mg
Dr. Pepper- 61 mg
Mountain Dew- 55 mg
Diet Dr. Pepper- 54 mg
Diet Coke- 49 mg
Pepsi Cola- 43 mg.

Take caution though when reducing caffeine especially if you consume a lot of it. Some people do have sensitivity to caffeine and might experience withdrawal symptoms such as headaches, and fatigue. If you drink five cups of coffee a day, you might want to start reducing that amount slowly over a period of a few months to reduce the withdrawal symptoms.

**Tip**
When you start to crave that coffee buzz, try pouring some sparkling water into your mug and sip on that. Keep sipping: most of us don't get enough water anyway.

## Nicotine

This is a strong stimulant that can play tricks on your mind. As an ex-smoker I can tell you it took a long time for me to realize that cigarettes were negatively contributing to my condition. I, like many smokers, often used smoking to calm my nerves when in reality nicotine does the opposite. Sure at first there is a calming effect, but that is more in your head. Nicotine speeds up your heart rate and can lead to more panic attacks and problems sleeping.

The hardest part about quitting are the withdrawal symptoms, especially if you quit cold turkey. If you quit cold turkey, you might find that your panic symptoms increase at least for the first week or so while the nicotine exits your system. This is due to your body's chemistry trying to correct itself and because of the mental withdrawal most smokers go through. I quit cold turkey and it was the hardest thing I have ever done, but I stuck to it. There are however many quit aids out that can help you make your quitting easier. There are nicotine replacement therapy drugs such as the nicotine patch, and nicotine gum that can slowly wean you off the nicotine. Then there are also some medications such as Zyban and Wellbutrin which are antidepressants that can help you with the withdrawal symptoms of quitting. While nicotine is not considered part of a diet, it does have to do with your bodies overall health and that is why it is included in this portion

## Sugar

We know that our bodies need sugar to survive. Sugar is our body's fuel. Our bodies need the naturally occurring sugar that is called glucose to provide us with energy.

However, how fast the glucose forms in your body can play an important role in our health. Most carbohydrates such as some breads, potatoes, vegetables, fruits and pastas contain starches that are slowly broken down into glucose while other foods that contain simple sugars like honey, white sugar and brown sugar along with candies break down quickly into glucose and overload us with it. Unfortunately almost all of us probably eat too much of this refined sugar daily because it is everywhere. It is in soft drinks, cereal, salad dressings, and even some meats. Studies have shown that the average person eats about 120 pounds of sugar a year. In some people this overload of glucose can lead to diabetes which is too high levels of sugar in the body, but it can also lead to the opposite when your blood sugar drops below normal levels. These people suffer from hypoglycemia. The symptoms of hypoglycemia strongly resemble the symptoms of a panic attack. If you suffer from hypoglycemia you might find yourself feeling light-headed, trembling, experiencing palpitations and even a more heightened sense of anxiety a few hours after eating a meal.

While there are some people who developed panic attacks from being hypoglycemic, it is not always the cause of panic attacks. Usually the hypoglycemia is just another issue that can bring on a panic attack. Correcting hypoglycemia is easy simply by making some big changes to your diet. You could start by cutting out all types of simple sugars from your diet. No more cookies, candy, soda, and ice cream to name a few. You will have to start reading the labels on your food to make sure they do not have high fructose either. Start eating more fruit but stay away from fruit juices as they are made with a lot of sugar. You also want to start eating more complex carbohydrates. Instead of eating pasta and white bread, add whole grain breads, brown rice, vegetables and even whole wheat pasta to your diet. Another adjustment is to add either a complex carb or protein snack between your meals. This should not be anything too big, but a few nuts or a slice of cheese will be enough to help keep your sugar level even.

Another way to help correct it, is by taking supplements such as Vitamin B-Complex and Vitamin C once a day with your meals. These will help increase your resiliency to stress. Stress can create blood sugar swings which can increase anxiety.

## Refined Carbohydrates

Cut down on refined and "white" carbs like white potatoes, white flour, white rice, and other refined carbohydrates that can cause blood sugar spikes. You should try to eat a balanced diet with plenty of fiber. Consume more whole grains, because they don't cause extreme spikes in blood sugar levels which can lead to low blood sugar.

Low blood sugar has symptoms that are very similar to anxiety. Symptoms include:
- Racing or palpitating heart
- Dizziness
- Trembling

- Weakness
- Anxiety
- Irritability

Many of these symptoms mimic the symptoms of panic attacks, and low blood sugar may be the catalyst that sets off attacks in some individuals. By cutting down on these "white" carb sources, you can help stabilize your blood sugar and reduce some of the symptoms that may trigger panic attacks.

## Stressful Eating Habits

How many times did you hear to chew your food growing up? I always thought my parents were just being difficult. I didn't think it mattered if my food was chewed or not because it was all going to the same place. Boy was I ever wrong. For years I had a habit of eating fast or grabbing something on the run and wolfing it down so fast I didn't even taste it. Because I ate so much and barely tasted my food, I often was still hungry and usually overate. Plus I was one of those people who needed to wash every swallow of my food down with something to drink (usually a soda). I always wound up with stomach pains and as embarrassing as it is to admit, some bad gas.

I never knew that if food is not chewed properly, it is not digested properly. So not only did I not taste my food, I was depriving myself of important nutrients in the food which was also contributing to me not feeling right all the time. I was always so stressed to get other things done that I never took the time-out to sit and really chew my food. My advice is when you eat, focus on the task at hand. Do not watch TV or read. Sit down at the table and leave when you are finished. Eat slowly consciously to give your stomach time to tell your brain when it's full. If you're still hungry after finishing your meal, wait 20 minutes before having a second helping or dessert.

The better you take care of yourself, the more likely you'll feel at your best!

## Changes You Can Make

The changes you can make to your diet are simple. Even if you are not hypoglycemic, you might still benefit from making the same changes as if you were hypoglycemic. Along with those changes you can also help reduce your anxiety by doing the following
- Eat more fresh and whole foods
- Eat more fresh fish and less red meat
- Increase your fiber intake
- Drink more water. Try to have at least 8 glasses of water a day
- Eat more vegetables.
- Make sure you eat balanced meals also.
- Chew your food!! Listen to your parents!

By making these changes to your diets, you will see a huge improvement in how you feel and how you handle stress.

## Get Rid Of Adrenaline

Adrenaline is a major cause of panic attacks. Some medical professionals believe that panic attacks may be caused by excess adrenaline in the system, or the body's inability to process adrenaline well.

You can get rid of excess adrenaline in your body by getting more exercise, punching a pillow, going for a walk, screaming into a pillow or any other aggressive, active method. When you get rid of the excess adrenaline, you will often find yourself feeling better very quickly.

# Chapter 9 - Talking To Yourself

If you suffer from an anxiety disorder, you are familiar with self-talk. Usually in the midst of a panic attack or any high anxiety moment, you find yourself being very negative. There are four types of self-talk that usually resemble a personality train that may be dominate in you.

## Tip:

Become an expert at recognizing your own automatic negative thoughts. Break down each anxious thought until it is very specific. The less vague your thoughts are, the easier it is to challenge them and reduce your anxiety.

## The Worrier

One of my favorite childhood authors Shel Silverstein wrote a poem in one of his books called "What if" and to this day it is my favorite poem. While some of the what if scenarios in his poems are a meant to be taken lightly (what if green hair grows on my chest) the rest of the poem is a classic example of a worrier trait. What if is the mantra for any worrier. Worries create anxiety by imaging the worst case scenario. If you fall into this category chances are you expect the worst, overestimate the odds of something bad happening and create images of failure. A typical self-talk for a worrier would be "Oh no my head is hurting. What if it is an aneurysm and no one can help me?"

## The Self Critic

You are your own worse critic. That is what I have always been told. Everyone has some insecurity that causes them to criticize themselves. Perhaps they feel their arms are too jiggle or their feet are funny. A critic however takes this a step further. If you are a critic, you are constantly judging yourself and your behavior. You feel like a failure because you are unable to handle your panic or anxiety disorder. The self-talk a critic usually takes part in is "what a disappointment you are, or you are stupid for feeling this way."

## The Victim

This is the part of you that feels helpless about your condition. You feel like it is incurable and you will always be this way. This is one of the most dangerous traits because it can leave you desperate. Recovery seems to be an unobtainable goal and this is usually what brings on depression. You will usually have thoughts like "I'll never be able to get control over this." and might even want to give up trying to get a handle on your attacks or disorder.

## The Perfectionist

Is very similar to the critic but instead of putting yourself down, you are driving yourself to do better. A perfectionist creates its anxiety by constantly telling itself that you should be working harder, or you should have everything under control. You have to please everyone and be nice to everyone no matter what they do or say to you. You have thoughts like "I have to get this job, or I have to be there for them when they call"

So can you experience all four types of negative self-talk? Can you be the worrier, the critic, the victim and the perfections all at once. Yes you most certainly can.

I was and some days I still find myself engaging in negative self-talk. When I started experiencing my anxiety I would always find myself saying "what if this is it? What if it is a heart attack?" As they grew more frequent I would find myself getting more depressed with each episode because I felt stupid for having those feelings and I thought I would never get a handle on it. I was pushing the man I was meant to marry away from me by not getting a handle on my attacks. I'm also a perfectionist. I have a hard time saying no to anyone and usually take on more than I can handle. I was the type of person who would put everything aside for someone else. If I had to say no to someone I felt like they would be furious with me for doing it.

One of the most beneficial things I learned when researching ways to manage my panic and anxiety was positive self-talk. It took a while and it feels funny at first, but it is something you will have to work at but the results are fantastic.

The first thing you need to learn to do is counter your negative self-talk with something positive. You might have to write down and rehearse saying these statements over and over again so you will believe them. Basically you are reprogramming all of your negative thoughts into positive thoughts.

As I said, this does take practice. Think about it though, it took us years to master our negative self-talk, and to undo all that will take some time and dedication. This was one of the hardest part of recovery for me. I have spent years from the time I was a teen engaging in negative self-talk. It was a habit that was hard for me to break.

One of the first things I learned to do to turn my negative into positive was to ask myself some questions. I wrote down on a piece of paper the following questions:
- Is this always true,
- Has this been true in the past, and
- What are the chances of this happening?

Here is how I began to apply it. When I felt a panic attack coming on and I had my first what if thought, my conversation with myself went something like this.

Oh my God I think I'm having a heart attack...
- Is this always true - I've thought I was having a heart attack many times in the past and I never was.
- Has this been true in the past - No it never has been true
- What are the chances of it really happening - After all the tests I have had done, I know I am healthy and my chances are small.

Every single time I felt my heart starting to pound I would go into the bathroom (which was my safe place) and have this conversation with myself. I would repeat this conversation for as long as the panic attack lasted.

Another thing I learned was to write down my positive statements and look over them all the time. I took situations that I knew might send me into a panic and wrote a positive statement about it. For example, I was afraid of elevators and getting stuck in one. Every time I stepped into an elevator my first thought was "what if this gets stuck and I have a panic attack?" I wrote that thought down and countered it by saying "I am confident and calm getting on the elevator".

It is important to avoid negative when writing positive statements which is why I didn't say "I will not panic getting on an elevator". The hardest thing for me was to believe in my statements. In fact some of the statements I originally wrote I had to change because I just didn't believe them. I had a journal full of negative statements that went through my mind everyday and I kept copies of these statements all over the place. I carried a copy in my bag at work so if I felt an attack coming on at work, I would grab my back and go look at my statements and repeat them out loud. As I progressed I found that I was able to change my statements into more positive statements because I believed it was working.

Another thing I learned to do was rationalize while I was having the panic attacks. Again this took a long, long, very long time to master. Every time I thought I was having heart attack and the feeling lasted for a while, I would keep repeating to myself that if I was having a heart attack it would have happened already. Or if I was having a stroke, it would have happened already. These thoughts and words helped me keep a clear head about the attacks and helped me identify the attacks even more.

The hardest part of my battle was recognizing the signs that an anxiety attack was coming on.

## Stress Building Personality Test

Here's a short stress building personality test you might want to take to assess your current stress state.

### Are You a Perfectionist?
- ✓ Do you feel constant pressure to achieve?
- ✓ Do you feel you haven't done enough, no matter what you do?
- ✓ Are you hard on yourself when you find out you're not perfect?
- ✓ Do you drive yourself to be the best in what you do, giving up every thing in the pursuit of perfection?

### Are You a Control Freak?
- ✓ Do you feel the need to be in control of everything and everyone?
- ✓ Do you think lack of control is a sign of weakness?
- ✓ Do you run your life by lists?
- ✓ Are you reluctant to delegate to others?

### Are You a People Pleaser?
✓ Do you need to have everyone like you?
✓ Do you feel upset if someone doesn't like you?
✓ Do you care more for others than you do for yourself?
✓ Do you hide your negative feelings so as not to displease others?

### Do You Feel Incompetent?
✓ Do you feel that you have poor judgment?
✓ Do you feel you lack common sense?
✓ Do you feel like an impostor?
✓ Do you feel that you don't do as good a job as others?

If you answer yes to any of these questions, you could have a potential problem there. More than two times yes in anyone area indicates a real roadblock.

## Blocking Behaviors Keeping Your Stress Alive

There are three obsessive behaviors that you are likely to be engaging in that impeded your healing process and stop you from enjoying a stress-free life. Recognizing these barriers can be a great first step toward getting rid of the problems that go with being too stressed.

The first is obsessive negativity. When you are obsessively negative, it means that you have a tendency toward being "negative" about people, places, situations, and things in your life. Perhaps you find yourself saying things like "I can't do this!" or "No one understands!" or "Nothing ever works!". You may be doing this unconsciously, but essentially you have what's known as a "sour grapes" attitude, and it holds you back from knowing what it's like to view life from a positive lens and enjoy the beauty in yourself and people around you! There's a whole world out there for you...with happiness and positive thinking.

Then you have obsessive perfectionism. When you engage in obsessive perfectionism, you are centered on trying to do everything "just so" to the point of driving yourself into an anxious state of being. You may find yourself making statements such as, "I have to do this right, or I'll be a failure!" or "If I am not precise, people will be mad at me!" Again, this behavior may be totally under the threshold of your awareness, but it interferes greatly with your ability to enjoy things without feeling "uptight" and "stressed."

Finally there is obsessive analysis. When you are obsessed about analyzing things, you find yourself wanting to re-hash a task or an issue over and over again. For instance, you might find yourself making statements such as, "I need to look this over, study it, and know it inside and out...or else I can't relax!" or "If I relax and let things go without looking them over repeatedly, things go wrong!" While analytical thinking is an excellent trait, if it's done in excess you never get to stop and smell the roses because you're too busy trying to analyze everything and everyone around you. Gaining insight into this type of behavior is one of the most important keys to letting go of stress, and getting complete power over your anxiety.

If you find yourself engaging in any of the above "Blocking Behaviors", there are two things you can do to help yourself. First, ask the people you know, love, and trust, "Am I negative about things?", "Do I complain a lot?", and "Am I difficult to be around?"

This may be hard for you to listen to, as the truth sometimes hurts a great deal. But the insight you will get from others' assessment of you is invaluable, and you'll know precisely how others see you. Accept their comments as helpful info, and know that you will gain amazing insights from what you hear. Second, keep a journal to write down and establish patterns of when you are using "blocking behaviors." Even if you are not thrilled with the idea of writing, you can make little entries into a note book or journal each day. The great part is that you'll begin to see patterns in your behavior that reveal exactly what you're doing to prevent yourself from curing your anxiety.

# Chapter 10 - Coping With Panic Attacks

Whether you suffer from panic attacks or anxiety attacks they are never fun and they can also be downright scary if you do not know what they are. This can be one of the most intensely uncomfortable feeling that you may ever experience and knowing that it can happen again without any warning can leave you feeling hopeless and helpless. If you have panic attacks, it may help to comfort you that you are not alone! You're not even one in a million. In America, it is estimated that almost 5% of the population suffer from some form of anxiety disorder. For some, it may be the occasional panic attack that only crop up in particular situations-like when having to speak in front of others, while, for other people, it can be so frequent and recurring that it inhibits them from leaving their home. But there is hope. There are ways that you can learn to cope with the attacks. You might even be able to make the attacks so insignificant they will no longer be a bother to you.

Some may not work for you, but others just might. It helps to know some of the most common coping techniques for dealing with panic attacks when they begin. Try them all and keep using the ones that work for you!

There are six changes you should could try to end the attack.
- Make it a regular routine to practice deep relaxation
- Do visualization exercises
- Develop a regular exercise program
- Cut down or out completely all stimulates from your diet
- Learn to express your feelings and accept them
- Turn Negative Self-talk into Positive.

Now all six of these will not work the same for every person. I never could get the hang of deep relaxation and while I managed to acknowledge my feelings, I still am learning each day how to express them.

## Deep Relaxation

An important step in overcoming panic attacks is to relax. That's easy to say but difficult to do. A good way to do this is to concentrate on your breathing making sure it is slow and steady. One of the first signs of a panic attack is difficulty breathing, and you may find yourself panting to catch a breath. When you focus on making those breaths even, your heart rate will slow down and the panic will subside.

Breathing more slowly and deeply has a calming effect. A good way to breathe easier is to let all the air out of your lungs. This forces your lungs to reach for a deeper breath next time. Continue to focus on your out-breath, letting all the air out of your lungs and soon you'll find your breathing is deeper and you feel calmer.

Ideally, you want to take the focus off the fact that you are having a panic attack. Try to press your feet, one at a time, into the ground. Feel how connected and rooted they are to the ground.

An even better way is to lie down with your bottom near a wall. Place your feet against the wall (your knees are bent) and press your feet one at a time into the wall. If you can breathe in as you press your foot against the wall, and breathe out as you release it, it will be more effective. You should alternate between your feet. Do this for 10 - 15 minutes or until the panic subsides.

Use all of your senses to take full notice of what you see, hear, feel, and smell in your environment. This will help you to remain present. Panic is generally associated with remembering upsetting events from the past or expecting something upsetting in the future. Anything that helps keep you focused in the present will be calming. Try holding a pet; looking around your room and noticing the colors, textures, and shapes; listening closely to the sounds you hear; call a friend; or smell the smells that are near you.

Many people strongly support aromatherapy to deal with panic and anxiety. Lavender can have an especially calming and soothing effect when you smell it. You can find essential oil of lavender at many stores. Keep it handy and take a sniff when you start feeling anxious. Try putting a few drops of lavender essence oil into some oil (olive or grape seed oil will do) and rub on your body. Keep a prepared mixture in a dark glass bottle for when you need it. You can even prepare several bottles, with a small one to carry with you.

Other essential oils known to help panic and panic attacks are helichrysum, frankincense, and marjoram. Smell each of them, and use what smells best to you, or a combination of your favorite oils mixed in olive or grape seed oil.

Another great tool to combating anxiety and stress is to use visualization.

## Visualization

The purpose of visualization is to enable you to quickly clear mental stress, tension, and anxious thinking.

The visualization can be used when feeling stressed and is useful when your mind is racing with fearful, anxious thinking. This visualization process, when practiced often, is effective for removing deep-seated mental anxieties or intrusive thoughts. To gain maximum benefit, the exercise must be carried out for longer then 10 minutes at a time, as anything shorter will not bring noticeable results.

There is no right or wrong way to carry out the visualization. Be intuitive with it and do not feel you are unable to carry it out if you feel you are not very good at seeing mental imagery. As long as your attention is on the exercise, you will gain benefit.

It is best to do this exercise in a quiet place where you won't be disturbed, and then when you are more practiced you will be able to get the same positive results in a busier environment such as the workplace. You should notice a calming effect on your state of mind along with a sensation of mental release and relaxation.

Either sitting or standing, close your eyes and move your attention to your breath. To become aware of your breathing, place one hand on your upper chest and one on your stomach. Take a breath and let your stomach swell forward as you breathe in and fall back gently as you breathe out. Take the same depth of breath each time and try to get a steady rhythm going. Your hand on your chest should have little or no movement. Again, try to take the same depth of breath each time you breathe in. This is called Diaphragmatic Breathing.

When you feel comfortable with this technique, try to slow your breathing rate down by creating a short pause after you have breathed out and before you breathe in again. Initially, it may feel as though you are not getting enough air in, but with regular practice this slower rate will soon start to feel comfortable.

It is often helpful to develop a cycle where you count to three when you breathe in, pause, and then count to three when you breathe out (or 2, or 4--whatever is comfortable for you). This will also help you focus on your breathing without any other thoughts coming into your mind. If you are aware of other thoughts entering your mind, just let them go and bring your attention back to counting and breathing. Continue doing this for a few minutes. (If you practice this, you will begin to strengthen the Diaphragmatic Muscle, and it will start to work normally leaving you with a relaxed feeling all the time.)

Now move your attention to your feet. Try to really feel your feet. See if you can feel each toe. Picture the base of your feet and visualize roots growing slowly out through your soles and down into the earth. The roots are growing with quickening pace and are reaching deep into the soil of the earth. You are now rooted firmly to the earth and feel stable like a large oak or redwood tree. Stay with this feeling of grounded safety and security for a few moments.

Once you have created a strong feeling or impression of being grounded like a tree, visualize a cloud of bright light forming way above you. A bolt of lightning from the luminous cloud hits the crown of your head, and that ignites a band of bright white light descending slowly from your head all the way down your body, over your legs, and out past your toes. As the band of light passes over you, feel it clearing your mental state. It is illuminating your mind and clearing any disturbing or stressful thoughts that you may have been thinking about. Repeat this image four or five times until you feel a sense of clearing and release from any anxious thinking. In finishing, see yourself standing under a large, luminescent waterfall.

The water is radiant and bubbling with vitality and life. As you stand under the waterfall, you can feel the water run over every inch of your body, soothing you

and instilling within you a sense of deep calm. Try to taste the water. Open your mouth and let it run into your mouth, refreshing you. Hear it as it bounces off the ground around you. The water is life itself and it is washing away stress and worry from your mind and body. After a moment, open your eyes.
Try to use all of your senses when carrying out the visualization.

To make the pictures in your mind as real as possible, use your senses of touch, taste, and hearing. Feel the water trickle down your body; hear the sound it makes as it splashes over you. The more realistic the imagined scenarios, the more benefit you will gain. Many people report useful and soothing results from using these simple visualizations often. The mind is much like a muscle in that, in order to relax, it needs to regularly release what it is holding onto.

You can use any situation or location that will help calm you. We like to call this "finding your happy place". Maybe you feel relaxed in a swimming pool or on the beach. Imagine yourself there. Just make sure wherever you go in your mind is a place where you can be calm and rested.

By visualizing the different situations, you are allowing your mind to release. It is like sending a message to your brain that when you close your eyes and begin this process it is time for letting go of anything that it has been mentally holding onto, including anxious thinking. To train your mind how to let go of the stress, it is important to practice this daily. With practice, you can learn to release all stress within minutes of starting the exercise.

Your daily practice should take place before going to bed, as that will enable you to sleep more soundly. Many people do not do these visualizations in the bedroom but some other room before going to bed. That way, when they enter the bedroom and close the door, they are leaving the mental stress and anxious thinking behind them. Just be sure you have the opportunity to concentrate on your mental images. Visualization as a tool for dealing with mental stress is very effective. If such visualization is carried out properly, you can reach a deep feeling of inner calm. This technique probably will not work in helping to end an anxiety attack, but it can help that attack from beginning. It is a powerful support tool for ridding yourself of general anxiety sensations.

With practice, you find you go days without having anxious thinking interrupt your life, and importantly, this significantly reduces the level of general anxiety you feel. Visualization is simply a tool you can use to overcome anxious thoughts and feelings.

**Positive Visualization**
Positive visualization can really help when both planning and dealing with holiday events and situations. Often, the expectation of things going wrong can produce more anxiety than the actual event or situation itself.

To combat this, try sitting quietly and comfortably with your eyes closed, breathing slow and even. If you like, perform one of the relaxation exercises outlined earlier before you begin.

Imagine a large, white screen in front of you and fill that screen with a picture of a forthcoming event or situation. Try to bring to your visualization all the color, sound and texture that you can.
Feel, see and hear what is happening. Make it really vivid and when your picture is as clear as possible, visualize yourself stepping in to that image. See yourself handling it – even enjoying it. Imagine yourself calmly and peacefully dealing with that situation or event. If you like, you can add what is known in NLP (Neuro-Linguistic Programming) as an anchor in the form of a small gesture such as a gently curled fist or a finger tap. Make this gesture as you visualize yourself confidently moving through the picture in front of you. Enjoy that sense of being able to handle things. Now open your eyes.
You may need to repeat this exercise a few times but ultimately it will work on your subconscious, dramatically reducing your expectant anxiety and therefore helping to ensure that the actual event or situation goes well for you. As a further boost, make that small gesture you came up with just before or as you enter the event or situation. This will work as a form of muscle memory, jogging your subconscious to remember that you are fine – that you can more than handle this.

## Breathing

The most important thing you should do whenever you experience a panic attack is to carefully control your breathing. Panic attacks can lead to hyperventilation, and can also be caused or exacerbated by hyperventilation. It's important to take slow, controlled breaths. Breathe in slowly, and then breathe out slowly. If you let your breathing get away from you, your anxiety is likely to skyrocket.

Panic attacks are often caused by, or made worse by physical conditions that scare you into believing something is medically wrong with you.

Hyperventilation can cause rapid heartbeat, chest tightness, and other symptoms that may feel like a heart attack. The fear of having a heart attack can cause panic attacks to get worse and worse. By breathing slowly and carefully, you can help slow down your respiration rate. You'll help keep your heart rate in check, and you will hopefully prevent the attack from spiraling out of control.

## Talk To A Friend

One of the quickest and easiest ways to reduce your stress is to talk to a friend. By simply calling them, you can begin to change the way you are thinking about your stress as well as how you might be reacting to it. You can either talk to your friend about the thing that is making you anxious or you can ask them to make you feel better about the stress you are feeling. No matter what your friend says, you will be able to reduce the anxiety you feel.

Just by asking for someone else's help, you will be able to increase the chances that you will begin to feel better quickly. People like to help other people, so tell your friend that you're upset and that you need them to help you distract yourself from the feelings you are feeling. Or you might want to pretend like nothing is wrong and let your friend talk about their life. Ask them questions and help them solve problems they might be having. This can often put your own problems into perspective and allow you to feel better about what you are doing. You might also want to ask your friend for advice on what you are doing (or not doing) at the moment.

If your friend is honest, they will show you any errors in your thinking and they might be able to offer you a fresh take on a problem you are facing – often showing you something that you missed because you were focused on your anxiety. Have someone on your speed dial that you can call when your anxiety is too much. Or you can always talk to their voice mail or answering machine.

## Deflate The Danger

A panic attack is a natural body reaction. When you have a panic attack or anxiety attack you are going through the same physiological flight reactions that you might in a life threatening situation. The number one difference is there is no immediate danger.

So why do people suffer from attacks if there is no danger? That is the million dollar questions that right now no one has the answer too. Some people believe there is always a reason for the attack while others believe that it can be caused from a temporary physiological imbalance. The only thing anyone knows for sure is that most people who suffer from anxiety have usually be dealing with long-term stress or have recently had a significant loss in their life.

Now since there is no immediate or at least apparent danger, you invent danger to explain the feelings we are having. If you are having heart palpitations your thoughts are "I'm having a heart attack or I'm dying". When you can't breathe, you might be thinking "I'm suffocating". I used to have headaches and a numbing sensation when I had an attack and I used to think "I'm having a stroke". It is these thoughts that make the panic attack grow stronger. I like to think of a panic attack as a monster and those thoughts were the food that made it stronger. The more food you feed it the stronger it gets until it controls your life and this was the point I was getting to until I learned to remind myself of a few key things.

The first thing I had to learn was that a panic attack does not and cannot cause a heart attack or cardiac arrest. It is a scary feeling though when you have heart palpitations and the first thing that will cross anyone's mind is a heart attack. I had to realize the sensations caused by these attacks are different from a heart attack. For starters my heart was racing, and pounding and it came and went in waves. It was never constant for a long period of time. Each time my mind said "heart attack" the feeling got worse. I would get chest pains off and on in the upper left side of my chest and sometimes moving around would help make these go away. he chest pain never lasted long. I never had a heart attack, so I didn't know what it felt like. I also sometimes made the mistake of reading online about heart attacks symptoms and saying to myself "Yep that is what I have right now", which made me only worse.

Finally after talking with my doctor he explained to me that with a true heart attack, there is continuous pain and pressure and even a crushing sensation in the center of your chest. I never experienced a crushing sensation in the center of the chest. Also with a heart attack some people report that these sensations might lessen if they rest and worsen if they move. I realized with a panic attack I felt worse when I tried to lay down and better when I was moving. Also during a heart attack, any abnormalities will be picked up by an EKG, and during a panic attack there are no abnormalities. It took three trips to the ER and a full work up from my doctor to show me that my heart was fine and that heart attacks in people with a healthy cardiovascular system were rare.

The next thing is that a panic attack will not cause you to stop breathing. It's not uncommon during an attack to feel like you are hyperventilating. This is partly because of the stress you might be under. That stress can cause the muscles in your chest to tighten and make it feel like you are suffocating. You will not stop breathing however. During a panic attack your brain will force you to breath because of a natural instinct. This is why you might find yourself gasping for breath throughout your attack.

Lastly, you will not go crazy during a panic attack. The fact that you think you may be going crazy is enough proof that you are not. Crazy people rarely are aware that they are crazy. Also going crazy does not happen as fast as a panic attack does. A crazy behavior that comes with mental illnesses such as schizophrenia develop over time. I never hallucinated or heard voices while I was having panic attacks but yet I was still convinced I was going crazy. It was the feeling of not understanding what was going on with my body that made me feel as if I was going crazy.

The thing I had to remember was that while not everyone has an anxiety attack, most people might experience some of the symptoms I did while I was having a panic attack. The difference is they did not look at those symptoms as anything dangerous. In fact a majority of people are able to identify these same symptoms as being signs that they are too stressed out.

So now that we know what the dangerous thoughts are how do we get rid of these thought? The first thing we need to do is recognize the signs of a panic attack. By just recognizing your tendency to believe that harmless symptoms are signs of danger is the first step. Once you are aware of these feelings and that they will cause you no harm, you will eventually stop having the thoughts of something dangerous or even fatal happening to you.

Next, write down alternative explanations of your symptoms. Think of how you feel when you are experiencing an attack and write down all your symptoms.

Then look at them and think of other explanations for them. For example automatically I thought heart palpitations = heart problems or attack. But once I started digging I realized that the heart palpitations can be caused by an outburst of adrenaline due to a potential situation. For example when my husband left me alone at night to go to work, my heart always started to pound as it got darker and later because in my mind there was a potential threat that something would happen to me. That is when my heart would start to pound and I would find myself not being able to breathe. If you find yourself getting dizzy or faint, this isn't because you are going to faint, but because of the increase in your blood pressure once you start feeling anxious or a little panicky.

Lastly, do not fight your panic attack when you are going through it. Fighting it only make it worse and ignoring it is the worse thing you can do. To overcome or at least be able to manage your panic attacks you need to face the symptoms and accept what your body is doing. When you try to fight against a panic attack, your body tends to tense up and make you feel even worse. Let your feelings go and allow your body to have the symptoms. You should already be able to recognize that you are experiencing a panic attack and you know all the alternative explanations for your symptoms. Think to yourself "Ok, here I go. I've been through this before and nothing bad has happened to me. This will pass, I'm just going to let my body do its thing and then move on. I've been through this before" and you will be amazed at how quickly your panic attack will pass as opposed to how long it seems to last when you are fighting it.
This ties into the positive self talk we talked about earlier. It takes some time and practice to recognize the signs of a panic attack and talking yourself through it is not something that happens overnight. I was able to pick up really fast when I was starting to have a panic attack, but trying to talk myself through it was very hard for me. I would say "Ok. You have been through this before and you were ok" but then another part of me would say "But what if this time is different? What if this is the real deal this time?". It took me a long time to realize that I can't go through my life thinking "what if?"
I had to tell myself it was not the real deal last time and chances are it is not the real deal this time. It was a long battle for me. There were times when I felt like I would never be able to manage my attacks and that I was destined to suffer from these for the rest of my life.

Another challenge is to find out what situations or circumstances can trigger your anxiety attacks. People who suffer from agoraphobia can identify their anxiety triggers a little easier. Some start when they have to drive over a bridge, or be in an enclosed space. Most of the time they will avoid those situations to avoid the panic attacks. Other people have spontaneous panic attacks that come out of the blue. I suffered from both. I knew what triggered my attacks from an agoraphobic point of few. However I suffered from the "out of the blue" attacks too.

If you find yourself suffering from what you think are out of the blue attacks there are some things you can do. First, keep track of their occurrences for at least two weeks. Keep an eye open for what was taking place right before the attack took place and what went on hours before it happened. Also ask yourself these questions:

1. Am I under stress?
2. Am I alone or with someone? If you are with someone ask yourself if they are a friend, family or stranger
3. How have I been feeling all day? What was my mood throughout the day?
4. Was I having any negative thoughts?
5. Am I tired?
6. Did I have a lot of caffeine right before everything happened?

These will help you identify a pattern leading to your attacks and what might trigger them. In my case, I noticed if I had a particularly trying day or had heard bad news, or became too overwhelmed with what I thought were my everyday responsibilities I tended to have an attack usually that night. I also noticed that if I was alone, I was more prone to any attacks. Perhaps my biggest trigger was when I thought about my father who had passed away suddenly two years ago. By not dealing with his death, and keeping my emotions inside, I somehow convinced myself that I was going to die just as he did. Alone and from a heart attack.

I was taught some key coping strategies to add to what I had already learned. One of them was to talk to another person when I felt the symptoms coming on. Mainly to me that person was usually my husband. Sometimes if I felt the attack starting I would simply tell him to tell me a story or to start talking about something, anything to take my mind off it. Sometimes I would do the talking and tell him how I was feeling and what was going through my head. For times he wasn't around and I felt an attack coming I would talk to whoever was around me. I started up random conversations with people in the elevator to get my thoughts off it stopping and me being trapped. I never told these people of my fears but just something as simple as "Its beautiful outside, isn't it" got my mind off my racing thought.

Another strategy that helped me out was to practice what some people call thought stopping. As soon as I felt the what if self talking in my head I would tell myself to stop or cut it out. If I was alone, I said these out loud and said it loudly. If I was around other people, I pictured the word stop. I would have to take a few deep breaths and constantly remind myself to stop the way I was thinking.

## Progressive Relaxation

Another very important technique for controlling panic attacks is through progressive relaxation. During progressive relaxation, you slowly begin relaxing your muscles a few at a time, envisioning your entire body slowly becoming limp.

Some people like to play relaxing music, nature sounds or brain entrainment sounds while doing this. It can help focus your mind to do this, but make sure you pick something that you enjoy and that helps you focus without being distracting.

Start by clearing your mind as much as possible. Try to focus on something that relaxes you. Think of your favorite vacation spot, your favorite hobby or someone you love. Imagine yourself happy and at peace. Close your eyes. Relax your facial and scalp muscles, taking care to pay attention to every muscle in your head. Make sure your scalp is relaxed, then your forehead is relaxed, then your cheeks, and so on.
Slowly move down to your neck, shoulders, and back. Feel a wave of relaxation spreading slowly through your body from head to toe, as if it were washing over you like a wave.
Relax your arms slowly from bicep down to your wrist. Move into your hands and fingers, relaxing each set of muscles separately. Let the wave wash down through your torso, your buttocks, your thighs and your calves.
Finally, relax your feet and toes. By now your entire body should be limp and completely relaxed.

Now you should stay in this state for a while. Try to focus on whatever got you centered in the first place. Imagine your calming place, your favorite happy thought or whatever else makes you truly calm and happy.

You can do this anywhere in some form. You may not be able to close your eyes and go completely limp, but you can use this technique anywhere to center your thoughts away from the panic attacks.

## Herbal Remedies

There are several herbal remedies than can help people with panic attacks. These are usually far cheaper than prescription medications, especially when you factor in the cost of the visit to the doctor to get the prescription.

KavaKava (also called kava kava) is a type of herbal tranquilizer that some people compare to Xanax in its power. It is indeed quite strong, but it doesn't seem to have the addiction potential of drugs like Xanax and Valium. Kava has been used for centuries by the Polynesians for ceremonies and as a general relaxer. In small amounts, it can make you feel generally well and happy. In larger doses, it can make you feel very tired and relaxed. Since kava is not addictive the way many other anti anxiety drugs can be, it can be taken fairly often. It also isn't believed to cause the kind of memory problems that some users experience with Xanax. If you have liver damage, kava may cause problems for you. It's not yet known exactly why, but kava doesn't seem to be safe in anyone who has liver issues. If you have liver damage, you should talk to a doctor before taking kava.

Valerian root is a herbal tranquilizer/sedative that has been in use in Europe for many years. It is used to treat mild to moderate anxiety, as well as insomnia.

Valerian is considered extremely safe, and you can take it daily for several months without any ill effects. As a precaution, I would take it only when needed. It does take several days or weeks of continued daily use to reach maximum effectiveness, but extended use may reduce its effectiveness. It's a bit of a paradox. Valerian comes in several forms. It can be bought in capsules, liquid extract or tea. All are effective, so just get whatever is available. One thing to note about valerian is the fact that it is very smelly. It smells very strongly of a wet dog. It is so strong that just touching a capsule can make your hands smell terrible for hours. It doesn't taste as bad as it smells and it doesn't make your breath smell bad, but the smell itself is terrible.

Passionflower can be found in capsule and liquid extract form and is a fairly potent tranquilizer. Some people say it is as potent as valerian. Passionflower can be combined with valerian, chamomile or other relaxing herbs safely, to maximize the effect of each of them.

Chamomile tea has been used for a very long time to help promote relaxation and sleep. It's not extremely potent, so it isn't likely to cause excessive drowsiness. That makes it perfect for use when you need to relax, but you don't need to sleep. Although it can help you sleep when you want to, it's probably not going to make you so drowsy that you end up falling asleep at the wheel of your car or at your desk at work. Chamomile, since it is so mild, is best used in conjunction with other herbal remedies. It can help enhance other herbs, but it isn't especially effective on its own.

## Music To Beat Stress

Listening to music does wonder to alleviate stress. Everyone has different tastes in music. We should listen to the music that makes us feel comfortable. Sitting down and forcing yourself to listen to relaxation music that you don't like may create stress, not alleviate it.

Music is a significant mood-changer and reliever of stress, working on many levels at once. The entire human energetic system is extremely influenced by sounds, the physical body and chakra centers respond specifically to certain tones and frequencies.

Special consideration should be given to the positive effects of one actually playing or creating music oneself. Among the first stress-fighting changes that take place when we hear a tune is an increase in deep breathing. The body's production of serotonin also accelerates. Playing music in the background while we are working, seemingly unaware of the music itself, has been found to reduce the stress of the workplace. That's why so many retail places play music while you shop – to take your mind off the high prices!

Music was found to reduce heart rates and to promote higher body temperature - an indication of the onset of relaxation. Combining music with relaxation therapy was more effective than doing relaxation therapy alone. Many experts suggest that it is the rhythm of the music or the beat that has the calming effect on us although we may not be very conscious about it. They point out that when we were a baby in our mother's womb, we probably were influenced by the heart beat of our mother.

We respond to the soothing music at later stages in life, perhaps associating it with the safe, relaxing, protective environment provided by our mother. Music can be one of the most soothing or nerve wracking experiences available. Choosing what will work for any individual is difficult, most will choose something they 'like' instead of what might be beneficial. In doing extensive research on what any given piece of music produces in the physiological response system, many unexpected things were found. Many of the so-called meditation and relaxation recordings actually produced adverse EEG patterns, just as bad as Hard Rock and Heavy Metal. The surprising thing was many selections of Celtic, Native American as well as various music containing loud drums or flute were extremely soothing. The most profound finding was any music performed live and even at moderately loud volumes even if it was somewhat discordant had a very beneficial response.

As we mentioned before, there is not a single music that is good for everyone. People have different tastes. It is important that you like the music being played. I recently picked up a rest and relaxation CD at Wal-Mart that has done wonders for me. It has the sounds of the ocean in the background while beautiful piano music plays. It's very soothing. One note here, it's probably not a good idea to play certain types of ballads or songs that remind you of a sad time in your life when you're trying to de-stress. The reason is obvious. You're trying to relax and wash away the anxious thoughts. The last thing you need is for a sad song to bring back memories you don't need anyway.

**Here are some general guidelines to follow when using music to de-stress.**
To wash away stress, try taking a 20-minute "sound bath." Put some relaxing music on your stereo, then lie in a comfortable position on a couch or on the floor near the speakers. For a deeper experience, you can wear headphones to focus your attention and to avoid distraction. Choose music with a slow rhythm - slower than the natural heart beat which is about 72 beats per minute. Music that has a repeating or cyclical pattern is found to be effective in most people. As the music plays, allow it to wash over you, rinsing off the stress from the day. Focus on your breathing, let it get deeper, slow and become regular. Concentrate on the silence between the notes in the music; this keeps you from analyzing the music and makes relaxation more complete.
If you need stimulation after a day of work, go for a faster music rather than slow calming music. Turn up the volume and dance! It doesn't matter if you can actually dance or not. Just move along with the music and do what feels good. You'll be shocked at the release you can feel!

When going gets tough, go for a music you are familiar with - such as a childhood favorite or favorite oldies. Familiarity often breeds calmness.

Take walks with your favorite music playing on the ipod. Inhale and exhale in tune with the music. Let the music takes you. This is a great stress reliever by combining exercise (brisk walk), imagery and music.

Listening to the sounds of nature, such as ocean waves or the calm of a deep forest, can reduce stress. Try taking a 15- to 20-minute walk if you're near the seashore or a quiet patch of woods. If not, you can buy tapes of these sounds in many music stores. This has been very calming for me – you should try it too!

There's another great relaxation technique that I have found in coping with my own anxiety problems: self-hypnosis.

## Self-Hypnosis For Stress

A few weeks ago, I was feeling particularly overwhelmed with stress and anxiety. It seemed like anything that could go wrong, did go wrong. I felt like I was spinning out of control. I happened to be writing a book on yoga and meditation at the time and came across a website that offered a downloadable mp3 hypnotic relaxation session. It cost me about $20 and it was the best $20 I have ever spent!

There are plenty of places on the Internet where you can get these downloadable sessions for a small fee. However, you can also practice self-hypnosis on your own. You first need to find a quiet place where you can fully relax and listen to your inner voice. You shouldn't try to make something happen. Let your mind listen and relax. A large part of achieving that hypnotic state is to allow it to happen naturally. Also, don't watch for certain signs or signals that you might be in a hypnotic state. We can guarantee that if you look for these signs, you won't be able to fully relax and gain the benefits of self-hypnosis. There are lots of different ways to experience hypnosis. No two people will have exactly the same experience. In one respect, though, everyone has the same experience: the hypnotic state is always pleasant! There are no "bad trips" in hypnosis. Keep in mind that self-hypnosis is a skill and that you will continue to get better at it and, as you do, it becomes ever more powerful.

It's a good idea to set up a schedule of practice, allowing yourself anywhere between 10 and 30 minutes, depending on how busy you are and how much time you have to spend at it. Practice during the best part of your day if you can and at a time when you are least likely to be disturbed by others. Most people find it best to practice lying down, in a comfortable position, with as few distractions as possible. If you are bothered by noise while you practice you can try to mask out the noise with some other source of sound. You can try stereo music in the background, or white noise if you like. If like most people you don't have a white noise generator, try tuning a radio receiver between stations. The static you get when you do that is similar to white noise. However this takes an older or cheaper FM receiver without a noise suppressor. Sometimes AM tuners can be used for this. This should just be in the background and not too loud to be distracting.

The basic divisions of a hypnotic induction are relaxation, deepening, suggestion application, and termination.

## 1. Relaxation

Your first job in the hypnotic induction is to slow the juices down and get yourself relaxed. But don't try to force your mind to relax (whatever that means)! If you get yourself physically relaxed, your mind will follow.

Relaxation – really deep relaxation – is an ability that most people have either lost or never developed. Some people can do it quite easily, though. They just let go of their tensions and let every part of their body become limp and relaxed. If you are one of these people, begin your self-hypnosis practice by getting nicely relaxed. Take your time. This is not something you want to rush.

The time involved for the relaxation phase of your self-hypnosis induction can vary from half an hour to just a few seconds. It is an important part of the induction and should not be slighted. As you get better and your skill increases you will recognize deeply relaxed states, and you will be able to achieve them in a surprisingly short time. But as a beginner, take your time. It will be time well spent.

A very popular method of deep relaxation is the Jacobson Progressive Relaxation procedure. This involves tensing each of the major muscle groups of your body (foot and lower leg on each side, upper leg and hip, abdomen, etc.). Tense the muscle group for a few seconds, then let go.

## 2. Deepening Procedures

Once you have completed the relaxation phase of your self-hypnosis induction procedure, you can begin to deepen the relaxed state. At some time between the deep relaxation and the deepening procedures you will move into a hypnotic state. You probably won't know it, especially as a beginner, but it will happen sooner or later. One of the first hurdles a beginner must get over is the compulsion to "watch for it." That is, you will keep waiting for hypnosis to happen, for some change in your awareness or the way you feel that will say to you, "You're hypnotized."

Watching for hypnosis will definitely get in your way if you don't get it out of your mind. Going into a hypnotic state is, in this respect, similar to going to sleep. If you try to catch yourself going to sleep – if you try to be aware of the precise instant in which you actually go to sleep – you are much less likely to go to sleep. "Watching" keeps you awake.

In this same way you will not know when you go into a hypnotic state (but that won't be because you lost consciousness – you won't). Later, after you have been practicing regularly for a few weeks or a month or two, you'll be much more familiar with yourself and how it feels to be hypnotized. Does it take everyone weeks or even months to get into a good hypnotic state? Definitely not. Some people have an amazing experience the very first time they try it.

Others might practice for several days, noticing nothing, then out of the blue they have one of those great induction sessions in which they know something stupendously good happened. But if you happen not to be one of these people, don't worry about it. Just keep practicing and you will eventually get there.

One of the most popular deepening procedures is the count-down technique. Hollywood also likes this one. That is why you see it in so many movies. That and the swinging watch.

To use the count-down technique you simply start counting downward from, say, 20 (or 100, or whatever). Adjust the countdown number to whatever feels right to you after you have practiced a few times. Imagine that you are drifting deeper with each count. Other images and thoughts will probably intrude themselves as you count. That is natural. Just gently brush them aside, continuing with your counting.

The speed with which you count down should be natural; not too fast, not too slow. For most people this means counting at a rate of about one count for each two or three seconds. Do it at a rate that feels comfortable and relaxed to you. Some people like to tie the count with their breathing. As they drift deeper their breathing slows down, so their counting also slows down. Don't count out loud, just think your way down the count. You want to avoid as much physical involvement and movement as possible.

**3. Suggestion Application in self-hypnosis**
Once you have reached the end of your deepening procedure you are ready to apply suggestions. What you have done during the relaxation and deepening procedures is increase your suggestibility. That is, you have opened up your subconscious mind at least a little bit to receive your suggestions. This works because of the particular, and peculiar, characteristics of the subconscious part of your mind.

The most common and easiest way to apply suggestions is to have them worked out ahead of time, properly prepared and worded, and memorized. It should not be too difficult to remember them because they should be rather short and you are the one who composed them. If you have them ready and remembered, you can simply think your way through them at this point. Dialogue, or more properly monologue, is also okay. You just talk ("think" to keep your effort to a minimum) to yourself about what it is you want to do, be, become, whatever. Don't say "you." You are thinking to yourself, so use the first person personal pronoun "I." Some suggestions can be succinctly stated in a somewhat more formal sort of way, like, "I am eating less and becoming more slender every day." Elaborated suggestions are generally wordier and more of an ad lib: "Food is becoming less important to me every day and I am filling my time with more important and meaningful pursuits than eating. It is getting easier and easier to pass up desserts and other fattening foods . . ." and so on.

Generally speaking, the most effective kind of suggestion is image suggestion. Image suggestions usually do not use language at all. You can liken this to seeing yourself in a calm, relaxed state while in the middle of a chaotic situation. Actually see yourself in your mind's eye.

Although people sometimes see immediate results from their suggestions, it is more likely to take a little time for them to kick in. So don't be impatient. On the other hand, if you have not begun to see some results within, say, a couple of weeks, you need to change your suggestions.

## 4. Termination
Once you have finished applying suggestions you are through with your induction and you can terminate your session. You could just open your eyes, get up and go about your business, but that is not a good idea. You should formally identify the end of every session. By doing this you provide a clear boundary between the hypnotic state and your ordinary conscious awareness. A clear termination also prevents your self-hypnosis practice session from turning into a nap. If you want to take a nap, take a nap. But don't do it in a way that sleeping becomes associated with self-hypnosis practice. If you are practicing at bedtime and don't care if you go on to sleep, that is okay. But still draw the line in your mind to indicate the end of your self-hypnosis session.

To terminate the session, think to yourself that you are going to be fully awake and alert after you count up to, say, three.
"One, I'm beginning to come out of it, moving toward a waking state. Two, I'm becoming more alert, getting ready to wake up. Three, I'm completely awake." Something like that.

Self-hypnosis can work wonders when it is practiced on a regular basis. You'd be amazingly surprised at the level of relaxation you can get to. It's one of the best things I ever did for myself!

## Yoga
Practicing yoga is a popular way of combating anxiety and its combination of physical and mental discipline really does help calm body and mind.

Yoga has many styles and forms – some more intense than others.
Hatha yoga, one of the most commonly available forms, is also one of the best for anxiety management. It is particularly popular with beginners because of its slower, easier movements and it is precisely these attributes that make it so suitable for anxiety sufferers. You can benefit, however, from almost any form of yoga although some dynamic forms, or styles such as Bikram yoga which is practiced in a hot environment, might not be as suitable if you suffer from an anxiety disorder. The most beneficial elements of yoga are controlled breathing and the focus away from everyday concerns as your body is taken through poses that require calm concentration. The increased fitness and resultant decrease in heart rate and blood pressure will also prove beneficial when managing anxiety.

Classes are widely available and it is a good idea to at least start learning with an instructor rather than from a book or DVD. You should, of course, consult your health care practitioner before starting classes if you have any major health concerns.

Taking a few moments away from the busy seasonal period to practice yoga is an excellent way to give mind and body a mini vacation from all that stress.

The combination of deep breathing and increased blood flow thanks to the poses will allow you to return to your routine refreshed and relaxed, allowing you to cope better with everyday concerns.

## Meditation

Meditating for twenty minutes daily can have a tremendous impact in all areas of your life. If you have a lot on your mind and you feel like your thoughts are driving you crazy, meditation can help you discover peace. Merely close everything, sit back, close your eyes, and clear your mind of every single thought. Center on the emptiness. You'll be surprised what a simple twenty minutes of meditation can do to turn things around for you.

If you have trouble meditating, I'd suggest getting a professional guided meditation CD, which will help you get used to this level of peacefulness.

### Breathing Meditation

Commonly, the purpose of breathing meditation is to calm the mind and develop inner peace. We can apply breathing meditations alone or as a preliminary practice to cut down our distractions before engaging in other types of meditation.

### An Easy Breathing Meditation

The 1st stage of meditation is to stop distractions and make our mind clearer and more coherent. This can be achieved by practicing a simple breathing meditation. We pick out a quiet place to meditate and sit in a comfortable position. We can sit in the traditional cross-legged posture or in any other position that's comfortable. If we want, we can sit in a chair. The most crucial thing is to keep our back straight to prevent our mind from getting sluggish or sleepy. We sit with our eyes partly closed and turn our attention to our breathing. We breathe naturally, preferably through the nostrils, without trying to control our breath and we attempt to become aware of the sensation of the breath as it comes in and leaves the nostrils. This sensation is our object of meditation.

We ought to try to concentrate on it to the exclusion of everything else. At the start, our mind will be very busy, and we may even feel that the meditation is making our mind more engaged; but in reality we're just becoming more cognizant of how busy our mind really is. There will be a great temptation to follow the different thoughts as they come up, but we should stand firm against this and stay focused single-pointedly on the sensation of the breath. If we detect that our mind has meandered and is following our thoughts, we ought to immediately return it to the breath.

We should repeat this as many times as necessary till the mind settles on the breath.

## Mantra Meditation
With this form of meditation you choose a calming word, thought or phrase and silently repeat it over and over. This helps push away other, more distracting thoughts and produces a profound sense of calm.
Transcendental Meditation is a form of Mantra Meditation and is highly recommended for those who suffer from anxiety.

## Mindfulness Meditation
This form of meditation may seem unusual in that, instead of closing your eyes and drifting away from your environment, you choose to become more aware of it and therefore more accepting.

This works by allowing you to accept thoughts or distractions and simply let them flow over you. Focusing on your breath and observing its flow helps you to achieve this state of relaxed mindfulness.

Mindfulness Meditation is particularly useful during hectic festivities or stressful occasions such as a Christmas party. You can do this without anyone even noticing, simply observing, accepting and letting everything flow over you while keeping your attention on your breathing until you feel calmer and in control.

## Walking Meditation
Another method which is well suited to helping combat seasonal anxiety as it allows you to withdraw from stress-inducing situations while also giving yourself a real physical and mental treat. During a walking meditation you adopt the principles of the Mindfulness Meditation in that you notice and appreciate everything around you as you pass by at a steady, even pace, concentrating on the motion of your legs and feet. You can even combine this with a Mantra Meditation, silently repeating a calming word, thought or phrase in your head as you breathe deeply and regularly.

The benefit of this kind of meditation is that you reap the rewards of both physical exercise and mental calming while giving yourself a proper psychological boost. This sort of 'me time' is vital during the festive season and particularly if you suffer from anxiety. Again, it need only be a few minutes, although 30 is optimum. Take a walking meditation a few times a week during the holidays and you will quickly start to see and feel the benefits.

## Back To Nature
We spend so much time captive in buildings of steel and concrete and bricks that we quickly blank out where we come from. It's natural for us to be in nature and this is why it feels so good and it is so peaceful when you take a walk in a park or bike on a trail in the woods.

## Get Back To Basic

As I'm typing this, I'm looking out my window to this mammoth tree in front of my house. Observing its stillness, with the wind blowing through its branches calmly, it's a sight that not only inspires me, but I find peace within it. If you feel overwhelmed, take a stroll outdoors where there are tons of trees and far from the city. Be there and simply enjoy the sights, the sounds and the peace.

Nature gives you a chance for unstructured exploration. Most people's lives are tightly scheduled and routine. Awaken, shower, commute, work, home, sleep. Every day you drive the same route, sit in the same cubicle, and sleep in the same bed. Yet inside each person is a strong urge to start out and explore, to begin a day with only the faintest outline of an agenda and to find things never seen before. Scrambling over rocks, hiking up mountains, and fording streams will make you feel like a child again. Nature gets you in touch with the common elements and your primal self.

The modern person is subject to all sorts of rules, anticipations and constraints. Clammed up and buried in paper work, he must act polite, follow the traffic laws, and abstain from throttling the a-hole who prolongs the company meeting with mindless questions. His spirit is constantly beleaguered. And everything modern man touches, lives in and uses has been altered from its original form: sanded, molded, and packaged for consumption. Almost every sound he hears, from the automobile engine to the ringing cellular phone, originates from an artificial source. It's enough to render every person with a mild form of insanity.

We need to have manners, but the primal side of us shouldn't be completely suffocated. We must periodically tear ourselves away from civilization and interact with matters in their state of nature. Touch real dirt, sit by a real fire, sharpen real wood and listen to the pure sounds of running currents and the wind in the trees. Encircle yourself with matter that doesn't exist entirely for human consumption. Feel things that just are.

Nature gives you space to think and puts your troubles in perspective. In the cities and suburban areas, it's easy to lose what is really important. The world begins to seem as if it truly does center on your tiny world. And there are few really quiet moments in this impulsive life. In the car you're listening to music or talk radio, at work you're centered on the project at hand, and when you get home you turn on the television set and zone out.

Getting lost in nature allows quiet, unstructured space in which to straighten out your problems, think through what's been going on in your life and design goals for the future. Under the stars and below the trees, it's easier to see what truly matters. Mountain peaks, rolling rivers, and radiant sunsets will make you and your problems seem decently small. Enlivens your body.

Every once in a while people must tear themselves away from the choked off air of the streets and the reprocessed air of corporate buildings. Your lungs ache to breathe the fresh air in the forests and mountains. Hiking will enliven your body. While all exercise is good for alleviating depression, outdoor exercise is especially useful.

The sunshine, physical activity and inspiring scenery will combine to rejuvenate your spirit and leave you ready to once again take on the world.

## Smile Power

Whenever you're laughing or smiling, something intriguing happens. Not only does something happen on a chemical level to make you feel better, but it besides stops all stress and negativity from entering your brain.

A simple smile can make such a difference. For instance, the other day I mishandled a dish and it fell down on the floor, breaking into bits, producing a big mess. Now, I could have been furious with myself for being clumsy and thinking "here's another reason why life is awful!" But I did the opposite. I began to smile and kind of make fun of myself for not being able to hold on to that plate correctly. As I cleaned up the mess, there was no bitterness or anger. As a matter of fact, I did it with a smile on my face...I executed it with peace. So if you find yourself in a similar quandary, just think of the bright side, and don't be shy to poke fun at yourself. You'll quickly realize that peace finds its direction much more easily to you when you smile.

### How to Smile, Even When You Don't Want To

#### Physical Technique.
The human body affiliates physical responses with the associated emotion. For instance, if you slouch a great deal, your body will naturally feel more sluggish as compared to a individual who maintains a beneficial posture. Likewise, even if you feel sad, you are able to still draw your lips together and gather up the ends to form a smile. You may find your mood bettering naturally. This method has helped me better my mood innumerable times.

#### Smile with your eyes.
This method involves concentrating your smile on your eyes rather than your lips. Think of your eyes smiling, or twinkling. You'll find that your entire face will have to lift itself to achieve this. You'll find your cheekbones lifting up and the tip of your lips lifting up to form a smile.

#### Emotional Technique.
Our emotional state is all in our frame of mind. As cliché as it sounds, you've got to want to be happy, in order to be happy. When you prefer to be happy, think happy thoughts. Consider a calm meadow; consider a loved one or a joke perhaps.

Remember, happiness is often a choice. Abraham Lincoln once remarked "most folks are about as happy as they make up their minds to be." We can decide to be happy or pitiful. Do choose happiness to fill your life. There's the expression "Smile and the whole world smiles with you." Well, expressions like this are really grounded in fact. When you smile, it does tend to touch off smiles in others around you.

Even in highly stressful situations, a smile can easily lighten up everyone's mood. The worth of a smile is priceless. It can't be purchased, solicited or borrowed. It costs zero to give, but is the most earnest gift that one may be able to give to another. A smile brings rest to the fatigued and is the best counter poison for discouragement. It imparts sunshine to the sad and hope to the hopeless. A smile is infectious. Start infecting individuals and winning friends with your smile now.

## Write It Down

Often, we tend to 'catastrophize' the stress we feel. We think that we have much more to worry about than we actually have. Of course, there are times when our worrying is justified. But if you find that your mind is racing and that you cannot concentrate because you are anxious, it can help to write down everything you are worrying about. You can use a special notebook or a plain legal pad to simply write down all of the tasks you need to complete or other things that are on your mind. This will help to separate your experience from the things that are weighing you down. By seeing your responsibilities in front of you, you will get a clearer idea of how you can tackle them – often in a less stressful way. Whenever you feel like you can't handle everything that's on your proverbial plate, write down what you're worried about.

You can take this one step further by writing down why these things worry you.
- I'm afraid I won't be able to do this right.
- I'm afraid I'll get fired.
- I'm afraid they won't like me anymore.
- I'm afraid that I will fail and end up living in a cardboard box.

Be as silly with your reasoning as possible because it will help you release your stress as well as realize that perhaps you're worrying needlessly. Some people find that writing down their worries at the beginning of the day gives them a better idea of what they need to do during the day to avoid stress, while others find writing down their worries at night allows them a chance to process potential solutions as they sleep.

## Distractions

For many people who suffer from panic attacks, they have to learn how to deal with stress and anxiety on a daily, even hourly basis. How do these people function without losing themselves in their stress?

### Distraction techniques
When you are feeling anxious, your body begins to react in a physical manner. And if you are already upset, you might feel these symptoms and begin to feel even more anxious.

What you need to do is to interrupt your stressful feelings so that you can focus on feeling better, instead of feeling worse. There are a number of ways to distract yourself when you are feeling the beginnings of anxiety or a full blown anxiety attack:

- Be observant - Look around you and find something to focus your attention on. Look at this item closely and try to find interesting things to examine.
- Count things - When you are in a setting that is upsetting, you can always count things around you to help take your mind off of your stress.
- Ask questions - Try asking someone a question that will take a long time for them to answer. This will give you something else to focus on, while also taking the spotlight off of you and your contribution.
- Play a computer game – Nearly every computer has pre-installed card games that you can play quickly without any loading time. Things like solitaire are fairly mind numbing and can keep your mind off of your panic just long enough to allow the physical symptoms to subside.
- Wash some dishes – If you're at home when the stress hits, try doing a mundane chore. Not only will you have accomplished something, but you will need to focus your attention on that chore in order to get it done right.
- Find license plates – Some people become nervous when they drive, but you don't want to lose your attention in this situation. Instead, try increasing your attention by looking for as many different license plates that you can. Make a game of it to keep your mind off of the possible things that could go wrong on the highway.
- Doodle – As simple as it sounds, doodling on a piece of paper can help you remove your attention from your stress and put it squarely on this simple and mindless task.
- Try affirmations – When you repeat to yourself that nothing bad is going to happen and that all is well, your body will begin to relax – even if you don't believe it completely.
- Try writing it down on a piece of paper whenever your stress levels begin to rise. Just as you can distract yourself and forget about a food craving you have, by taking a few moments to distract yourself from stress can help you avoid an anxiety attack or just a moment of panic.

## Plan!

Too often, when we are stressed, organization and planning get avoided. While this seems like a good idea as you feel that you don't have time to do one more thing, you might actually be increasing your stress by not taking control in these simply ways.

When you organize your desk, it's easier for you to find things, which can immediately decrease your anxiety levels. You've probably already found this to be true. So, when you are under a lot of stress, you should stop and clean up your work area in order to allow yourself to feel more in control – because you will be. At first, this might actually make you feel more stressed as you uncover things that you don't necessarily remember having to do, but as you begin to create an organization system, you will feel more on top of the things you need to accomplish.

Here are some simple organization and planning tips that will help you find a system that works best for you:

- File folders – When you have things that you need to organize and complete on a certain schedule, it can help you to have a few file folders to organize it all. Some people like to have certain colors of folders for certain priority levels. For example, if things are very important and need to be done today, they might go in the green folder. Or if you can do them later, they can go into a yellow file folder. And as you complete all of the things in the green folder, you can move to the other folders.
- Have a tiny 'in' box – Instead of simply throwing things in piles around your home or office, you should have an 'in' box that will hold all of the things that need to be addressed. But the trick with this is that as soon as you get new things to put into this box, you need to deal with it. It should be sorted into a file folder, thrown out, or filed in a cabinet, if necessary. This will help you keep your 'To Do' list manageable, plus it will help you tackle the most important things first.
- Use a calendar – It doesn't matter if your calendar is a paper calendar or a high tech PDA, make sure you are writing down the things you need to do and when they need to be done by. This will help you see when you need to say no to new projects or when you might need to ask for help in order to get things done on time. If you want, you can also create quicker deadlines for yourself to help you ensure things get done on time.

What you are doing when you create an organization system is to empty your mind of the things you need to do.

Once you have a system in place that you trust, you can let go of the anxiety you have surrounding whether or not you're on track – you will already know.

## Showers And Other Strange Fixes

When you are trying to quit a certain habit, some psychologists recommend replacing the habit with something that's unrelated to the previous habit. For example, if you want to give up snacking between meals, experts recommend keeping your hands busy. The same kinds of tactics can be applied to your anxiety. No matter where you are, there are things you can do that are in complete opposition of your rising stress, helping you change anxiety into something more positive. And the more you change your thinking from panic to calm, the more quickly you will be able to get yourself out of a stressful mindset in the future.

Try some of these fun and strange fixes:

- Take a shower – When you are feeling anxious, your body tends to tense up and produce knots that make you feel worse than you already feel. Instead of letting your body tighten up, try taking a shower to loosen your body up. Not only will the hot water help your tension, but a shower is also a place where you can be completely alone with your thoughts. Have special soaps that smell good or a waterproof radio to turn your shower into a secrete getaway.
- Craft time – If you are artistically inclined, or even if you're not, try finding a craft you would like to do whenever you are feelings stressed. Even a simple coloring book can help you divert your attention from stressful feelings and help you feel relaxed. Maybe you can make holiday cards when you are feeing stressed or you can take out a piece of clay and sculpt it.
- Laugh – Whether you talk to a friend who is always funny or you stop to watch a recording of your favorite comedy, take a few minutes to laugh and smile. You don't need to be slapping your knee in order to get stress relief, but simply making your body feel good will help to counteract the stress you are feeling. You simply can't feel stressed when you are smiling.
- Play with a child or a pet – Since you don't want to be upset around either a pet or a child, you will help to reduce your stress immediately. You can find your own fun stress reducing activities too. Figure out what makes you happy and feel better and then make sure to practice it regularly.

## Keep Hope Alive

Hope is something you can never afford to lose.

### Look Forward

With hope you forever have a path towards peace. If we get too stressed out and overwhelmed within our own life, we blank out that hope. We blank out that the sun always shines after a rainy day and that this is simply a bump in the road.

I find immense peace in just recognizing, deep within my heart, that everything will be all right. With hope, I understand that whatever is apparently dreadful is only impermanent and that in time, things will be just fine. This takes off all of that negativity from my total being and pretty much immediately I feel better. I learned that hope is the sole option. Without hope I have zero. Hope isn't "wishful thinking" of the "if wishes were horses" assortment.
Hope is the most potent force in the universe. Hope is faith—in spirit, nature, science, and mankind.
What matters is having hope in the future—hope that we'll wake up tomorrow to a better day. Hope is the future—the only future worth having.

Few of us seem to feel the need for encouragement when matters are going well. Think of the baby boomers and the "me" generation of the 1970s. It's as if the party was never going to end. When times are hard, the success that many of us took for granted seems elusive and momentary. But, you can keep hope through these hard times.

## How To Remain Hopeful In Bad Times

- Bear no expectations. Do something you love, and do it on a lark. Anticipate nothing in the least, positive or negative.
- Aim your personal life back on track. Reconnect with the things that interest you. Teach your child something this weekend. Look up that old acquaintance from school. If you've gotten on cruise control as a multi- tasking, people pleaser, now may be a beneficial time to do a course correction.
- Place the past in its right perspective. The past was great, wasn't it? Or, was it? A few of us are in danger of OD'ing on nostalgia. Let go of the past. Not the individuals and places, but what could be your glamorized version of the past. Even if it was as good as you recall, you can't remain hopeful about the past.
- Extend. Find other people like you, they're out there. They may have been right in front of you, while you were busy twiddling with your cellular phone. Explore your neck of the woods. Find new places for socializing. If you're newly jobless enjoy the luxury of this time.
- Don't put your eggs in one basket. Forever have something else to look forward to, or better yet a lot of somethings. Whether it's a side business, exchanging friendly e-mails, meeting with friends or discovering a fresh hobby. Never depend upon any one part of your life for your hopefulness.
- Unwind. If you follow at least a few of these steps routinely, you're on a path to eventual success. You already have a leg up on becoming more peaceful because you have the right attitude. After all, optimism and hopefulness are such precious commodities in today's world.

## Live For Today

Most of the time, what we worry about is bearing on to something either in the past, or something that hasn't happened.

### Be Present

Living in the here and now erases all such thoughts. Why worry about something in the past that we can't ever change? Why worry about something that we're not even sure will happen or not? This is why in the here and now, you find true inner peace. In the present moment, there are no troubles and no concerns. There's only stillness, and it's within that stillness that you can expose peace.

I used to be such a person that worried day in and day out, to the point where I had difficulty sleeping. When people suggest that I "live in the moment" I understand the concept and can realize the value. But I secretly wonder, "How on earth do you really do that?"

I spent one of the last glorious days of summer lazing on the beach with a dear friend. We were relishing in the final rays of the afternoon sun when the conversation turned to his single status. He shared with me that an old lady friend, currently married, was possibly about to be single again. Acknowledging he had a "thing" for this woman in the past and a want-to-be in a relationship now, I was all over the "potential" that they may yet wind up together. Feeling his overt lack of exuberance over my colorfully painted vision of his future, I asked him what was up; to which he answered, "I don't live in the past or the future, I live in the moment".

"Live in the moment? What the heck does that mean? How do you do that?" I retorted, with plenty of exhilaration in my voice. He told me he didn't know how he did it, he just did.

As afternoon fleeted into evening his answer stayed with me. I started wondering why I so automatically move out of the present and into the future. I put myself in his shoes and envisaged how I may deal with the same state of affairs.

I ascertained that I leave the present and go into the future to protect myself. If I run all the conceivable scenarios through my mind, good or bad, and "prepare" myself for what may be, I figure, fore warned is fore armed? Correct? Well, perhaps not.

Now, let this be said, I'm not stating planning's a bad thing, or daydreaming for that matter. But it doesn't escape my notice that a lot of the future "proposing" I do isn't peaceful.

Here are some hints I've learned that help me stay a bit longer in the here and now.

- When you discover yourself envisaging fearful scenarios ask yourself, "Is this the only hypothesis?" Search for what else could be true, instead of what you fear.
- Remind yourself that worrying about the time to come or regretting the past isn't going to change what has or is going to happen.
- Do you have a profound trust that whatever happens you're going to be ok? Can you discover times from your past that serve as grounds that this is true? If so, draw on that experience.
- Are your basal needs met, does your life work? Often we move into the future as we think it will be better there. Think about addressing what ever isn't in balance so it will become suitable to be more in the now.
- Practice the mightiness of the present. Centre on something positive or beautiful right here and now and breathe it in. Let yourself amply feel it.
- Then, be willing to let go of that also and march on to the next moment.

# Chapter 11 - Stress Management

As we've said before, stress is a part of life. There's no getting away from it. In fact, some stress is good stress. You may not believe that, but sometimes stress can motivate us to do things we may not normally do in a relaxed state. Stress can make us brave enough to go forward when normally we might hesitate.

We have to be resilient in order to effectively cope with stress and help it enhance our life instead of control it. How do you get strong and resilient? By learning how to take control of your stress and make it work for you instead of against you.

Recognizing stress symptoms can be a positive influence in that we're compelled to take action – and the sooner the better. It's not always easy to discern why you have the stress in each situation but some of the more common events that trigger those emotions are the death of a loved one, the birth of a child, a job promotion, or a new relationship. We experience stress as we readjust our lives. Your body is asking for your help when you feel these stress symptoms.

We're going to give you many suggestions in this chapter. Not all of them will work for you, but we're willing to bet that some of them will.

There are three major approaches to manage stress.
**The first is the action-oriented approach.** In this method, the problems that cause stress are identified and necessary changes are made for a stress free life.
**The next approach is emotionally oriented** and in it, the person overcomes stress by giving a different color to the experience that caused stress. The situation, which causes stress, is seen humorously or from a different angle. I especially advocate this approach to stress management. Sometimes if you don't laugh at a situation, you'll cry – uncontrollably. That's no solution. So learn to see the humor instead of the doom.
**The third way is acceptance-oriented approach**. This approach focuses on surviving the stress caused due to some problem in the past.

The first stress management tip is to understand the root cause of your stress. No one understands your problem better than you do. A few minutes spend to recognize your true feelings can completely change the situation. During this process, identify what triggered the stress. If someone close to your heart is nearby, share it with the person. If you are overstressed and feel you are going to collapse, take a deep breath and count till ten. This pumps extra oxygen into your system and rejuvenates the entire body. When under severe stress meditate for a moment and pull out of the current situation for a little while. Stand up from your current position and walk. Stretch yourself. Soon you will find that the stress has lessened. This is because you have relaxed now and relaxation is the best medicine for stress.

Smiling is yet another way of stress management. If you are at the work place, just stand up and smile at your colleague in the far corner. You will see a change in your mood.
Learn some simple yoga or mediation techniques.

You can also invent your own stress management tips. The basic idea is to identify the cause of stress and to pull out from it for a moment and then deal with it. Taking a short walk and looking at objects in nature is another stress reliever. Drinking a glass of water or playing small games are simple stress management techniques. The whole idea is change the focus of attention and when you return to the problem, it does not look as monstrous as you felt before.

Here are some quick steps you can take toward relieving stress:

## 1. Don't just sit there. Move!
According to many psychologists, motion creates emotion. You might notice that when you are idle, it's easier to become depressed. Your heart rate slows down, less oxygen travels to your brain and you are slumped somewhere in a chair blocking air from reaching your lungs. I challenge you right now, regardless of how you are feeling, to get up and walk around at a fast tempo. Maybe you might want to go to an empty room and jump up and down a little bit. It may sound silly but the results speak for themselves. Try it now for a few minutes. It works like magic. Exercise can be a great stress buster. People with anxiety disorders might worry that aerobic exercise could bring on a panic attack. After all, when you exercise, your heart rate goes up, you begin to sweat, and your breathing becomes heavier. Don't panic – it's not an attack! Tell yourself this over and over while you're exercising. Realize that there's a big difference between the physical side of exercise and what happens when you exercise.

## 2. Smell the roses.
How do you smell the roses? How about investing some money to go on that one trip you've been dreaming about? Visit a country with lots of exotic places to jolt your imagination and spur your creativity. You need to detach from your daily activities and venture a little bit.

## 3. Help others cope with their problems.
It is very therapeutic when you engross yourself in helping others. You will be surprised how many people's problems are worse than those you may be facing. You can offer others assistance in countless ways. Don't curl up in your bed and let depression and stress take hold of you. Get out and help somebody. But be careful. Don't get caught up in other people's problems in an attempt to forget about your own. Friends and family are constantly calling me when they want to vent or get advice. I joke and tell them "Don't call the 'crazy' person for advice!" But there are times that I find myself worrying about the ones who call me and I get caught up in what they're going through. This just gives me more stress than I already have and I find that I have to step away and re-assess

myself and my priorities. I'm now to the point where I can tell them that I just can't deal with it right now and to call back later. Sometimes, they get upset, but more often than not, they understand. But I've learned not to get too upset about their reactions. If it won't matter in a week, it should matter right now.

### 4. Laugh a little.
By now you've heard that laughter is a good internal medicine. It relieves tension and loosens the muscles. It causes blood to flow to the heart and brain. More importantly, laughter releases a chemical that rids the body of pains.
Every day, researchers discover new benefits of laughter. Let me ask you this question: "Can you use a good dose of belly-shaking laughter every now and then?" Of course you can. What you are waiting for? Go to a comedy club or rent some funny movies.

### 5. Wear your knees out.
If there were one sustainable remedy I could offer you when the going gets tough, it would be prayer. Many people, depending on their faith, might call it meditation. It doesn't matter to me what you call it, as long as you have a place to run to. There you have a few quick fixes when you're feeling stressed. Want more? No problem!

### 6. Make stress your friend.
Acknowledge that stress is good and make stress your friend! Based on the body's natural "fight or flight" response that burst of energy will enhance your performance at the right moment. I've yet to see a top sportsman totally relaxed before a big competition. Use stress wisely to push yourself that little bit harder when it counts most.

### 7. Stress is contagious.
What we mean by this is that negative people can be a huge stressor. Negativity breeds stress and some people know how to do nothing but complain. Now you can look at this in one of two ways. First, they see you as a positive, upbeat person and hope that you can bring them back "up". If that's not it, then they're just a negative person and can't feel better about themselves unless those around them are negative as well.
Don't get caught up in their downing behavior. Recognize that these kinds of people have their own stress and then limit your contact with them. You can try to play stress doctor and teach them how to better manage their stress, but be aware that this may contribute more to your own stress, so tread lightly.

### 8. Copy good stress managers.
When people around are losing their head, who keeps calm? What are they doing differently? What is their attitude? What language do they use? Are they trained and experienced? Figure it out from afar or sit them down for a chat. Learn from the best stress managers and copy what they do.

### 9. Use heavy breathing.

You can trick your body into relaxing by using heavy breathing. Breathe in slowly for a count of 7 then breathe out for a count of 11. Repeat the 7-11 breathing until your heart rate slows down, your sweaty palms dry off and things start to feel more normal.

## 10. Stop stress thought trains.

It is possible to tangle yourself up in a stress knot all by yourself. "If this happens, then that might happen and then we're all up the creek!" Most of these things never happen, so why waste all that energy worrying needlessly? Give stress thought-trains the red light and stop them in their tracks. Okay so it might go wrong – how likely is that and what can you do to prevent it?

## 11. Know your stress hot spots and trigger points

Presentations, interviews, meetings, giving difficult feedback, tight deadlines........ My heart rate is cranking up just writing these down! Make your own list of stress trigger points or hot spots. Be specific. Is it only presentations to a certain audience that get you worked up? Does one project cause more stress than another? Did you drink too much coffee? Knowing what causes your stress is powerful information, as you can take action to make it less stressful. Do you need to learn some new skills? Do you need extra resources? Do you need to switch to de-caffeinated coffee?

## 12. Eat, drink, sleep and be merry!

Lack of sleep, poor diet and no exercise wreaks havoc on our body and mind. Kind of obvious, but worth mentioning as it's often ignored as a stress management technique. Listen to your mother and don't burn the candle at both ends! Avoid using artificial means to dealing with your stress. That means don't automatically pour a glass of wine when you think you're getting stressed out and don't light up a cigarette. In actuality, alcohol, nicotine, caffeine and drugs can make the problem worse. A better idea is to practice the relaxation techniques we've given you. Then, once you're relaxed, you can have that glass of wine if you want.

## 13. Go outside and enjoy Mother Nature.

A little sunshine and activity can have amazing ramifications on your stress level and will enhance your entire outlook towards life. Your improved attitude will have a positive effect on everyone in your family and/or circle of friends; things which seem overwhelming will soon become trivial matters, causing you to wonder what the predicament was. Not only will you be less stressed, you will be healthier, happier, and more energetic; ready to face whatever obstacles come your way.

## 14. Give yourself permission to be a 'kid' again.

What did you enjoy when you were a child? Draw; paint; being creative. Play with Play- dough, dance or read. Play music, allow yourself freedom to express yourself without worrying that you're not keeping with the image of who you are 'supposed' to be. Just relax and enjoy yourself. We all have a little child in us and it's a good idea to allow expression of the child within from time to time. If

I might say so, this suggestion is excellent and very therapeutic. I speak from experience. I can tell you there is nothing more satisfying than buying a brand new box of 64 Crayons – the one with the sharpener in the box – and coloring away in a coloring book.

## 15. Don't set unrealistic goals for yourself.
Many of us set ourselves up for defeat simply by setting unrealistic goals for ourselves. For example, if you are dieting, realize you cannot lose 40 pounds in one or two months. Or maybe you are trying to reach a goal of obtaining a particular job position; whatever your goal is allow sufficient time to reach your goals and realize occasional setbacks may occur. If you reach your goal without any delays, you will be even happier with yourself for arriving quicker than you planned, but don't expect it. In fact, don't expect anything; expectations and reality are often two entirely different things.

## 16. Learn it is OK to say 'no' occasionally.
Often, many of us feel we have to say 'yes' to everyone, every time we are asked for help and feel that we must respond in a positive fashion. But, remember, you cannot be all things to all people. You must first meet your own needs before you can truly give others what they need while at the same time keeping yourself happy.

## 17. You do not have to do everything your family, friends, and others ask.
Of course you can help others, but first make sure you have done what is necessary to take care of yourself.

## 18. Make time for yourself, your number one priority.
Once your own needs are met you will find you have more time for others. And you may find more pleasure in helping others when you don't feel that you must always put others needs before your own. We're not done yet!

There are so many great ways to combat stress and anxiety. You deserve to get all the information you can. Here's some more stress busters.
I really love this thought and have used it many times myself!

## 19. Yell!
That's right, scream at the top of your lungs – as loud as you can. While this may not be feasible in your home, it works great when you're in your car with the windows rolled up. Let out a guttural yelp from deep down inside. It's liberating!

## 20. Sing.
As we said in the previous chapters, music can be extremely beneficial when getting rid of stress. Think how much better you can feel when you belt out "Copacabana" at the top of your lungs! Who cares if you can't carry a tune? You're doing this for you!

### 21. Take up a new hobby like knitting or crocheting.
Don't worry about being good at it. It's the process that's beneficial. Sitting still while performing repetitive movements is calming and stabilizing for many people. It can be time to collect your thoughts.

### 22. Start a garden.
Even apartment-dwellers can do this. Inside in pots, pots on the patio, a small spot in your yard. There is a little work to setting it up. Tending plants, fruits, vegetables, flowers and watching them grow, bloom or yield food is rewarding. Avid gardeners say working a garden is the best way to control stress and worry. An added benefit is the creation of a more beautiful, restful environment.

### 23. Play with a dog or cat.
Experts say pet owners have longer lives and fewer stress symptoms that non-pet owners. Playing with your pet provide good vibrations – for you and for the pet! It's a form of social interaction with no pressure to meet anyone's expectations!

### 24. Look at the stars and the moon.
It can be a very humbling experience to lay on a blanket with your hands behind your head and gaze up into the night sky. It's more than humbling; it's downright beautiful and relaxing! When you look at the vastness of the sky, you realize that our problems are small compared to that. I also get great comfort from seeing that one bright star in the sky that is always above my house. When my best friend's mother died, we got out of the car after coming from her visitation and my friend's five-year old and I stopped to star gaze. She pointed out one particular star and said "That's my grandma. She's our guardian angel now." Every time I see that star, I know Cheryl's there and she'll help get me through anything!

### 25. Treat yourself to some comfort food.
But be careful or over-eating could become your big stressor. Enjoy in moderation and make yourself feel better. I love mashed potatoes and gravy and macaroni and cheese. Those are my comfort foods. But I make sure that I don't overdo it. I give myself just enough to bring on that calming feeling.

### 26. Swing.
Remember the feeling of sitting inside that little piece of leather on the playground as you sway back and forth and feel the wind whipping through you hair? Do that! If you don't have a swing in your yard, go to a playground and remember to pump your legs back and forth to see how high you can go. It's liberating!

### 27. Take a candle lit bubble bath.
Even you guys out there can benefit from a warm bath in the soft glow of candlelight. Lay your head back, feel the bubbles and the warm water and let your stress go right down the drain when you pull the plug! Phew!

There you have twenty-seven ways to relax and de-stress! You can come up with your own ways as well! The key, really, is to find something that makes you feel better when you are overwhelmed and practice that method faithfully. You'll be a healthier person overall.

# Chapter 12 - Just Say No

Setting adequate boundaries is another essential if you are to get through the seasonal period unscathed. Always remember that it is OK to say no. If you don't want to go to that big office party then say so and similarly if you cannot face another family dinner or gathering.

It is far worse to say yes and then feel your anxiety build as you force yourself to attend an event you are not enjoying. Forget about people pleasing – it is more important to please yourself so that you can stay calm and relaxed. Another huge problem people who are overly stressed out have is the ability to say "No" when they need to. Maybe your mother wants you to take Grandma to the store, but you're in the middle of a big work project. Perhaps your best friend asks if you wouldn't mind babysitting her kids when you've already made plans with yourself to get a haircut.

There's no reason why you have to say "Yes" to everyone. In fact, there are often many times when you should turn them down. If you find yourself agreeing to do things when you really don't want to, you're a people pleaser. In general, this isn't a bad trait to have, but it can be a huge stressor. People pleasers think of other people's needs before their own. They worry about what other people want, think, or need and spend a lot of time doing things for others. They rarely do things for themselves, and feel guilty when they do. It's hard being a people pleaser. People pleasers hold back from saying what they really think or from asking for what they want if they think someone will be upset with them for it. Yet they often spend time with people who don't consider their needs at all. In fact, people pleasers often feel driven to make insensitive or unhappy people feel better - even at the detriment to themselves. Constantly trying to please other people is draining and many people pleasers feel anxious, worried, unhappy, and tired a lot of the time. They may not understand why no one does anything for them, when they do so much for others - but they often won't ask for what they need.

This is the trap I fell into. I found myself always agreeing to do things for others but when I needed those same people to help ME out, they were curiously occupied.

A people pleaser may believe that if they ask someone for help and that person agrees, that person would be giving out of obligation, not because they really wanted to. The thinking goes - if they really wanted to help, they would have offered without my asking. This line of thinking happens because people pleasers themselves feel obliged to help and do not always do things because they want to. Sadly, people pleasers have been taught that their worth depends on doing things for other people. It's painful being a people pleaser – believe me, I know!

People pleasers are not only very sensitive to other people's feelings, and often take things personally, but they also rarely focus on themselves. When they do take a moment for themselves, they feel selfish, indulgent, and guilty which is why they are often on the go, rushing to get things done. Because people pleasers accomplish so much and are easy to get along with, they are often the first to be asked to do things - they are vulnerable to be being taken advantage of. People pleasers were most likely raised in homes where their needs and feelings were not valued, respected, or considered important. They were often expected as children to respond to or to take care of other people's needs. Or they may have been silenced, neglected, or otherwise abused, thus learning that their feelings and needs were not important. In many cultures, girls are raised to be people pleasers - to think of others' needs first, and to neglect their own.

Many women have at least some degree of people pleasing in them. Men who identified with their mothers often do as well. People pleasers' focus is mostly on others and away from themselves. They often feel empty, or don't know how they feel, what they think, or what they want for themselves. But it's possible to change this pattern and to feel better about yourself.

I managed to learn how to break out of this cycle. You can do the same thing if you see yourself in the description above. You want to know how? It's easier than you think!

First, practice saying NO. This is a very important word! Say it as often as you can, just to hear the word come out of your mouth. Say it out loud when you are alone. Practice phrases with NO in them, such as, "No, I can't do that" or "No, I don't want to go there".

Try it for simple things first, and then build your way up to harder situations. Stop saying YES all the time. Try to pause or take a breath before responding to someone's request. You may want to answer requests with "I need to think about it first, I'll get back to you" or "Let me check my schedule and call you back". Use any phrase that you feel comfortable with that gives you time before you automatically respond with YES.

Take small breaks, even if you feel guilty. You won't always feel guilty, but most likely in the beginning you will. Remember that your mental health is well worth the aggravation you may have to take from others. What's important is you. When you are healthy, those around you will be healthy! Figure out what gives you pleasure. For example, you may like reading magazines, watching videos, going to a park, or listening to music. Give yourself permission to do those things and then enjoy them. Ask someone to help you with something. I know this is a hard one but you can do it! After all, everyone else is asking you for favors, why shouldn't you ask them?

Just be tolerant if they turn you down. Just because you have always told them "Yes" doesn't mean they always have to tell you "Yes". Check in with how you feel and what you are thinking. It's important to be aware of these things; they're part of who you are. And then try saying what you feel and think more often. Just remember to have a little decorum in certain situations.

Many people pleasers believe that nobody will like them if they stop doing things for other people. If someone stops liking you because you don't do what they ask, then you're being used by them and probably don't want them as a friend anyway. People will like you for who you are and not simply for what you do. You deserve to take time to yourself, to say NO, and to take care of yourself without feeling guilty. It's within your reach to change - one small step at a time! I think most people would be in complete agreement when I make this next statement.

McDonald's had it right – You Deserve A Break Today!

# Chapter 13 - Take A Break

So often, we know inside ourselves that we need a break. That break might be a full-fledged vacation or a weekend getaway. Either way, getting out of the daily grind can be amazingly liberating and a huge way to get rid of stress and anxiety.

Unfortunately, many people think they can't take the time to get away. This is toxic thinking. Get out and get away!

How many times have you continued working, knowing that you are not giving 100% to the task at hand? How many times have you read or written the same sentence over and over again, as your mind keeps wandering and thinking about other things? How often have you wanted to take a break from the family or kids but feared the consequences of doing so? It's time for a break!

Why do we not allow ourselves the time to take a 'time out'? Perhaps we feel like we don't deserve it or that there's just too much to be done. There are many genuine reasons for needing to complete jobs and tasks; however we may also on occasion have 'hidden agendas' as to why we cannot stop for a break.

Why? It could be ego. Some people simply enjoy boasting about, 'how late they had to work in order to complete a project' or 'how much effort they invested in order to complete the job so quickly'. This type of person is often looking to impress others with their efforts, thereby increasing their ego in the process.

Maybe you think you just can't take the time off. "I can't stop; I just have to get this finished". Does this sound familiar? "I can't stop because the job has to be finished,

Why? So I can move straight on to the next thing, and the next, and the next etc..." This person will find that there is always something that has to be done, which will constantly prevent him/her from taking a break. Maybe you just feel like you need to be needed. A mother managing the household, kids and other chores may feel as if her household will collapse if she were to put her feet up or take a weekend off! By not taking a break she can keep convincing herself that her role is crucial and the family would collapse without her input. This may indeed be true, but is still not a good enough reason to prevent her from having a rest!

Get rid of that thinking! You can get some amazing benefits just by taking a little time for yourself! Allowing your mind and/or body to rest can help re-focus your attention, sharpen your wits and increase motivation. In addition, taking time out helps to relieve stress, can aid the recovery of tired muscles and also promotes the discovery that there is more to life than just work.

Many athletes will tell you that an important part of their training routine is rest. Muscles need time to repair after a workout. Remember that your brain is a type of muscle as well. It needs time to rest and recuperate in order to perform at its best. By giving your brain time off, you'll be able to concentrate better and give tasks you once found difficult your full attention. They'll be easier, believe me!

So you've decided that a break is in order. Good for you! A break can be anything from a 10-minute meditation session to a trip around the world, and anything in-between. I think a break should be something that takes your mind off a preoccupation with the everyday tedium of life.

So depending on the time you wish to avail towards relaxing, you may enjoy reading, watching a movie, cooking, playing with the kids, riding a motorbike or driving, exercising or doing sports, traveling or simply sleeping!

While you are taking this rest, above all, allow yourself the time to do it and don't feel guilty about. You will gain so very much by this time off, so enjoy the time you are giving yourself. Life will go on without you and contrary to what your mind might be telling you, everyone will survive – even when you're not there!

Let everything go and concentrate on you for once instead of everyone around you! If you're feeling tired, unmotivated or just in need of a rest, don't be a martyr or look negatively at this. You may actually find that in reality, allowing yourself a break will actually help you ultimately become more efficient and effective in every part of your life. Plus you'll get the badly needed recharging of your "batteries" that you sorely deserve! Work can probably be one of the most stressful places to be. You might think that none of these techniques can help you when you're around your co-workers. You couldn't be more wrong.

# Chapter 14 - Relaxing At Work

Coffee breaks aren't the only times when you can take a moment for yourself. Experience has actually taught me that coffee (or smoke) breaks can actually add to the stress you feel when you're at work. Some of the suggestions we've given you in this book can certainly be practiced at work, but, unfortunately, others cannot.

Here's a tried and true method to help you relax at work.

First and foremost, find a place to sit. Sit up straight with your back against the back of your chair, your feet flat on the floor, and your hands resting lightly on your thighs. If possible, close your eyes. You may do the exercise without closing your eyes, but closing your eyes will help you relax a bit more. Do not clench your eyes shut. Let your eyelids fall naturally.
Breathe in slowly through your nose, counting to 5.
Hold the breath for a count of 5.
Breathe out slowly, counting to five.
Repeat.

This exercise is performed by tensing and holding a set of muscles for a count of 5, and then relaxing the set of muscles for a count of 5. When you tense each muscle set, do it as hard as you can without hurting yourself. When you release the hold, be as relaxed as possible.

Begin by tensing your feet.
Do this by pulling your feet off the floor and your toes toward you while keeping your heels on the floor.
Hold for a slow count of 5.
Release the hold.
Let your feet fall gently back.
Feel the relaxation.

Think about how it feels compared to when you tensed the muscles.

Relax for a count of 5.
Next tense your thigh muscles as hard as you can.
Hold for a count of 5.
Relax the muscles and count to 5.
Tighten your abdominal muscles and hold for a count of 5.
Relax the muscles for a count of 5.

Be sure you are continuing to sit up straight.
Tense your arm and hand muscles by squeezing your hands into fists as hard as you can.
Hold for a count of 5.
Relax the muscles completely for a count of 5.

Tighten your upper back by pushing your shoulders back as if you are trying to touch your shoulder blades together.
Hold for a count of 5.
Relax for a count of 5.
Tense your shoulders by raising them toward your ears as if shrugging and holding for a count of 5.
Relax for a count of 5.
Tighten your neck first by gently moving your head back (as if looking at the ceiling) and holding for 5.
Relax for 5.
Then gently drop your head forward and hold for 5.
Relax for a count of 5.
Tighten your face muscles.
First open your mouth wide and hold for 5.
Relax for 5.
Then raise your eyebrows up high and hold for 5.
Relax for 5.
Finally clench your eyes tightly shut and hold for 5.
Relax (with eyes gently closed) for 5.

Finish the exercise with breathing.

Breathe in slowly through your nose, counting to 5.
Hold the breath for a count of 5.
Breathe out slowly, counting to five.
Repeat 4 times. And that's it!

Perform this exercise whenever you need to relax, whether it's on a plane or in a car or anyplace else you may be sitting. Because this exercise may be very relaxing, it should not be performed while driving. Over time, if performed regularly, this exercise will help you recognize tension in your body. You will be able to relax muscles at any time rather than performing the entire exercise. Perform at least twice a day for long-term results. You may develop your own longer relaxation exercise by adding more muscle groups. Pinpoint your own areas of tension, then tense and relax these areas in the same way. Maximize the relaxation benefits of this exercise by visualizing a peaceful scene at the end of the exercise. Visualize a scene - a place where you feel relaxed - in detail for at least 5 minutes. Remember the happy place? Go there and enjoy it!

# Chapter 15 - Exercise, Exercise, Exercise...

Successfully dealing with your anxiety does not happen overnight. I took baby steps and first learned to tell the signs of a panic attack. Once I had that down, I tackled my negative thoughts. It did not take me a year to start feeling better though. I started feeling better once I was able to identify the signs of an attack. I also learned how to manage my stress and one of the most helpful things was an exercise program.

An exercise program is one of the most effective methods for reducing stress and anxiety. There are many benefits to a good exercise program

•Production of endorphins that increase your sense of well-being
•Improved circulation
•Improved digestion
•A rapid metabolism of excess adrenaline in the bloodstream
•Helps reduce problems sleeping
•Can reduce depression
•Can reduce stress and anxiety also

One of the biggest problems most people face today is having no outlet for their stress. Usually you might wind up taking it out on people who are close to you. While there are other things you can do such as beating a pillow, exercise however seems to be the number one solution to reducing your stress.

**Caution:**
If you're over 35 or in poor physical condition, don't start an exercise program before you see a doctor for a physical exam and a treadmill test. Before you even start an exercise program you have to assess your fitness level so you know what program to choose. See if you have any symptoms of being out of shape. Some of them are being out of breath every time you walk up a flight of stairs and you have a hard time catching your breath from it. Does basic exercise exhaust you? Also look at how active you are. How often do you work out and for how long? If the answer is hardly ever, you will probably benefit from an exercise program! Now I know you are excited, but are you really ready for an exercise program? If you have never had an exercise routine before, you want to meet with your doctor to make sure you have no underlying factors that could be aggravated with exercise. You should especially see your doctor for a physical if you are over 40 and not used to much exercise.

**Choosing An Exercise program**
There are so many programs out there, that everyone should be able to find a program they can do and stick with. Most of the time you should look at what you want to get from exercise to help decide what program to stick with. Aerobic exercise is great for reducing generalized anxiety and panic attacks. This exercise requires the use of your larger muscles and is great for your cardiovascular condition. This is the capacity of your circulatory system to deliver oxygen to your tissue and cells. A good aerobic exercise program can

110

consist of any of the following; running, walking, cycling either outdoors or on a stationary bike, swimming, dancing and kickboxing. You can also look into a good strength training program to gain muscle strength.

Strength training can help tone your muscles and give you a leaner look. If you want to socialize and meet people then you should try to engage in a cardio workout like racquetball. You can even take up golfing though it is not a cardio workout, it is a great stress reliever. The week before our wedding, my husband and I spent the afternoon at a golfing range just to get all the stress from the wedding off our chests. It was the best day out we had in a long time.

**Tip:**
Too much exercise all at once will simply pile on more stress than you need. Start slowly, and gradually increase the length and difficulty of your exercise.

Another good idea is to have your exercise program outside. Sometimes just the fresh air can help clear your head and give you a better sense of perception. You can do running, walking, biking, hiking and even gardening outside. For me, I needed an aerobic workout that was going to be an outlet of my stress and help me sleep at night. My best friend had recommended kickboxing and I was hooked after my first class. Being able to punch and kick at imaginary people was just what I needed to get my pent up stress out, though I would recommend if you are new to exercise, you take it slow if you go the kickboxing route. Besides kickboxing, I am a big walker. I love to walk, whether it is walking around outside on a beautiful day or doing laps around my local mall.

Walking is the most highly recommended exercise not only for managing stress but also for losing weight. It is easy to do and does not require any special equipment and the risk of hurting yourself is slim.

**Getting Your Program Started.**
So now that you have an idea on what you want to do, how should you start? Assuming you have never exercised before you have to start slow. If you start off to hard-and-fast from the beginning you are going to burn yourself out. Here are some guidelines if you have never exercised before. Start off slowly. Most doctors will tell you that if you have never exercised before you should start off exercising for 10 minutes every other day for at least the first week. Then with each passing week, add 5 more minutes to your routine until you reach about 30 minutes. You should also give it a trial of one month.

Most people who have never exercised before will experience some discomfort those first few weeks. You may feel achy and sore and find yourself having a hard time pushing yourself to do the exercise. However most people say that after the first month they start to experience enough benefits to motivate them to keep on going.

Speaking of achy and sore, expect this! The saying goes "No pain, no gain". The soreness you may be feeling is a sign that you are doing it right and stretching your body the way it needs to be. Making it a habit to warm up before you begin will help reduce some of the soreness you will feel the next day. After a vigorous workout, make sure you give yourself a cool down. If you are working out on a machine in the gym, you will see that most machines such as the elliptical and treadmill will automatically factor in a five-minute cool down where they will lessen the intensity. Even if you are not on a machine, you should still remember to do a cool down. If you were jogging, spend a few minutes when you are done walking around to bring the blood back from your muscles to the rest of your body.

While some people use exercise to help them sleep at night, it is not a good idea to exercise less than two hours before you go to sleep. Your endorphins have been kicked into overdrive and you may find yourself too wound up to sleep. Most people enjoy working out first thing in the morning to get their energy up for the day.

### Using Exercise To Help Reduce Anxiety

When you are using exercise to reduce anxiety, keep these points in mind. Your exercise should be ideally aerobic and you should aim at doing your exercise 20-30 minutes at least 4-5 times a week. Aim to hit your target heart rate for at least 10 minutes during your routine. To figure out your target heart rate this is the formula to use (220-your age) x .75.

You can use the following chart

Age - Heart Rate
20-29 | 145-164
30-39 | 138-156
40-49 | 130-148
50-59 | 122-140
60-69 | 116-132

Lastly, avoid exercising only one time a week. When you do spurts of exercising you are adding more stress to your body and it is doing more harm than good. However say you can only make it to the gym once that week, you should walk for the rest of the week.

### Overcoming Excuses For Not Exercising

Exercise, we all have excuses for avoiding it. I am guilty of it myself. Some of the most common excuses I have are I don't have the time, I'm too tired, exercising is boring, it's a pain to have to go somewhere to exercise and what if I have a panic attack while I'm exercising.

**I don't have the time to exercise** is the number one excuse most people use when it comes to exercising. I've even used this one several times. I thought there was no way possible I could take 30 minutes out of my busy day to exercise. I felt there were more important things to do then to exercise. The reason why I had no time to exercise was because I never was willing to make the time. There were so many little changes I could have made to give me the time. Instead of spending 20 minutes in the morning picking out my outfit for the day and ironing it, I could do it the night before and use those 20 minutes to workout. Instead of coming home on my lunch hour and sit and watch TV, I could walk around my building for a half hour.

It wasn't until I realized how important exercise was to managing my attacks that I began to make these changes.

**I'm too tired to exercise.** This is another one of my favorites and more common if you are going to exercise at the end of the day. How many times have you skipped the gym because you were too tired at the end of the day. What you might not know is that exercise can overcome tiredness and that if you exercise regardless of how tired you feel, you will find yourself feeling reenergized afterwards!

**Exercise is boring.** There are some people out there than can get bored doing the same activity over and over again, which is why they are given a number of options on what exercise to do. Maybe the one exercise you have been doing is boring so have you tried others? How about trying a work out buddy? I think one of the reasons why I enjoyed kickboxing so much was because I did it with a friend. I even liked going to the gym more if I went with someone. If no one is around, try switching up your routine. Some days walk, other days pop in a video and do that. There are some fantastic exercise videos out there. With all the options there are out there for a good exercise routine, you should never find yourself bored.

**It's a pain to have to go somewhere to exercise**. You do not have to belong to a gym to get a good workout. I said before there are hundreds of exercise videos out on the market today. You can do everything from kickboxing to walking in the comfort of your own home. There is also a great demand for exercise equipment. Think about buying a bike or a treadmill to use. If you think you might get bored from that, place the exercise machine in front of the TV and work out to that. Or keep a radio nearby. We had an exercise machine and I would plop in a DVD and watch that while I worked out. I would get so caught up in what I was watching that the 30 minutes flew by.

If you don't want to spend the money on exercise equipment or videos, just turn on your radio and dance your heart out for a good 20 minutes or so!

**What if I have a panic attack?** Jumping into a tough program when you have never exercised before might well create the same symptoms of a panic attack, but a nice brisk walk will not. If you start to feel uneasy or you are losing control, stop and wait until you compose yourself before continuing. Talk to yourself and realize that you are not having a panic attack out of the blue, it is just your body's normal response to the exercise you are not use to.

Exercise is an important part of recovery and managing your anxiety. The benefits of exercise are not only going to help you manage your anxiety and your stress better, but the other health benefits far outweigh any excuse you may have to get out of it.

**Exercise**

Starting or keeping to a suitable exercise routine during the holidays will bring many of the same benefits as you can experience from yoga and walking meditation.

Whether you choose to practice a martial art such as Tai Chi or QiGong, both excellent for combating anxiety or instead prefer jogging or the gym, the trick is to work within your personal limits and to listen to your body. Pushing yourself too hard will only stress you even more and will counteract many of the benefits of exercise.

The direct anxiety-relieving benefits of exercise are that it is:
1. Mood boosting – Regular exercise increases self-confidence and improves sleep, which is often disrupted by stress or anxiety.
2. Endorphin producing – Physical activity boosts production of the brain's feel-good neurotransmitters which are known as endorphins.
3. Calming - As a meditation in motion, the focus on a single activity takes you away from everyday stresses and cares. While shedding tension and engaging in the task at hand, you also experience the increased energy and optimism that comes with physical activity.

# Chapter 16 - Use The Tools You Have

No one expects you to wake up one morning and discover you are "cured" of your panic attacks. You should however try to carry out some of the ideas mentioned here, especially if you do not want to take any medication.

Anxiety is not something to be ashamed of. It is a problem that affects more people than you might realize. I always thought I was the only person who was going through it and now I am finding all sorts of people who suffer from anxiety in one form or another.
Some of them are on medication and some of them took the same route I did to manage their attacks.

It's been nearly 3 years since I started having panic attacks. I am nowhere near cured, as my last panic attack was back in May, but I was able to identify it and deal with it so quick that it did not even affect me. If I can learn to manage my panic attacks and anxiety, then so can you. Now take that important first step

PS: Treat yourself with the utmost kindness and respect during what is often a trying time for many people. Give yourself the gift of self-care and enough space so that you can remain as anxiety free as possible. If you do experience symptoms, don't beat yourself up but simply use one of the techniques given to you in this report to soothe and ultimately overcome your anxiety. Remember that repetition of a technique or exercise on a regular basis will yield the best results. I wish you a calm, happy and anxiety free life and I know you can do it.


.....Riverside, CA, USA, October 2011
.....Maarheeze, Netherlands, November 2011

# Chapter 17 - DSM

## DSM IV

The Diagnostic and Statistical Manual of Mental Disorders (DSM) is published by the American Psychiatric Association and provides a common language and standard criteria for the classification of mental disorders.

It is used in the United States of America and in varying degrees around the world, by clinicians, researchers, psychiatric drug regulation agencies, health insurance companies, pharmaceutical companies, and policy makers. The DSM has attracted controversy and criticism as well as praise.

There have been five revisions since it was first published in 1952, gradually including more mental disorders, although some have been removed and are no longer considered to be mental disorders, most notably homosexuality.

The manual evolved from systems for collecting census and psychiatric hospital statistics, and from a manual developed by the US Army, and was dramatically revised in 1980. The last major revision was the fourth edition ("DSM-IV"), published in 1994, although a "text revision" was produced in 2000. The fifth edition ("DSM-5") is currently in consultation, planning and preparation, due for publication in May 2013.

Many mental health professionals use the manual to determine and help communicate a patient's diagnosis after an evaluation; hospitals, clinics, and insurance companies in the US also generally require a 'five axis' DSM diagnosis of all the patients treated. The DSM can be used clinically in this way, and also to categorize patients using diagnostic criteria for research purposes. Studies done on specific disorders often recruit patients whose symptoms match the criteria listed in the DSM for that disorder.

## DSM 5

The next (fifth) edition of the American Psychiatric Association's (APA) Diagnostic and Statistical Manual of Mental Disorders (DSM), commonly called DSM-5 (previously known as DSM-V until the APA decided to abandon the Roman Numerals), is currently in consultation, planning and preparation. It is due for publication in May 2013 and will supersede the DSM-IV which was last revised in 2000.
APA has an official development website for posting of draft versions of the DSM-5
http://www.dsm5.org/pages/default.aspx

Among the revisions considered is the proposal to make Agoraphobia a separate, codable diagnosis rather than occurring solely within the context of Panic Disorder.

Furthermore, Panic Attack is not a codable disorder, but the work group has proposed criteria for the assessment of Panic Attacks.

## DSM-IV & DSM-IV-TR CAUTIONARY STATEMENT

The specified diagnostic criteria for each mental disorder are offered as guidelines, because it has been demonstrated that the use of such criteria enhances agreement among clinicians and investigators. The proper use of these criteria requires specialized clinical training that provides both a body of knowledge and clinical skills.

These diagnostic criteria and the DSM-IV Classification of mental disorders reflect a consensus of current formulations of evolving knowledge in our field. They do not encompass, however, all the conditions for which people may be treated or that may be appropriate topics for research efforts.

The information presented in this book is not meant as a substitute for diagnosis or professional advice. It is merely a presentation of information concerning Anxiety Disorders and should not be used to self diagnose or treat individuals with Anxiety Disorders. If you suspect a person as having an Anxiety Disorder or other health problems, please contact a qualified medical practitioner.

# Reference

## External links

Anxiety Disorders Association of America. Information for families, clinicians and researchers http://www.adaa.org
National Institute of Anxiety and Stress. Information and treatment options for individuals http://www.conqueranxiety.com

## Bibliography

Antony, Martin, (2004) 10 Simple Solutions to Panic: How to Overcome Panic Attacks, Calm Physical Symptoms, & Reclaim Your Life, New Harbinger Publications, Canada, ISBN 1572243252
Bourne, J. Edmund (2005), The Anxiety & Phobia Workbook, New Harbinger Publications, Inc. Oakland, ISBN 1-57224-413-5
Bourne, J. Edmund (20012) Beyond Anxiety & Phobia, New Harbinger Publications, Inc. Oakland, ISBN 1-57224-229-9
Buell, Linda Manassee (2001),Panic and Anxiety Disorder 121 Tips, Real -Life Advice, Resources & More, Simplify Life, Poway ISBN 1-926507-04-7
Carbonell, David Ph.D (2004) Panic Attacks Workbook. A Guided program For Beating the Panic Trick Ulysses Press, Berkeley ISBN 1-56975-415-2
Frish, Noreen Cavan, Frish, Lawrence E. (1998) Psychiatric Mental Health Nursing, Delmar Publishers, Albany ISBN 0-8273-7233-7
Joppen, Ruud & Leeuwen, Guido Van, (1990), Stress Herkennen, Hanteren en Verwerken, Uitgeverij Kosmos, Utrecht/Antwerpen, ISBN 9021515881
Lenson, Barry (2002) Good Stress, Bad Stress: An Indispensable Guide to Identifying and Managing Your, Marlowe & Company, new York, Marlowe & Company ISBN 9781569245293
Patmore, Angela (2006) The Truth About Stress Atlantic Books, London ISBN 1843542358
Sterk, Fred & Swaen, Sjoerd (2001) Leven met een paniekstoornis, Bohn Staflue van Loghum, Houten/Mechelen ISBN 9031335614
Turkington, Carol A. (1998) Stress Management for Busy people. McGraw-Hill, New york. ISBN 0-07-065535-9
Vanin, John & Helsley, James (2007), Anxiety Disorders: A Pocket Guide For Primary Care, Humana Press, ISBN 978-1-58829-923-9

CPSIA information can be obtained at www.ICGtesting.com
Printed in the USA
LVOW13s0951180813

348440LV00004B/374/P